people in the NEWS

Brett
Favre

by Terri Dougherty

LUCENT BOOKS

A part of Gale, Cengage Learning

GALE
CENGAGE Learning

Detroit • New York • San Francisco • New Haven, Conn • Waterville, Maine • London

GALE
CENGAGE Learning™

LIBRARY OF CONGRESS CATALOGING-IN-PUBLICATION DATA

Dougherty, Terri.
  Brett Favre / by Terri Dougherty.
      p. cm. — (People in the news)
  Includes bibliographical references and index.
  ISBN 978-1-4205-0124-7 (hardcover)
  1. Favre, Brett—Juvenile literature. 2. Football players—United States—Biography—Juvenile literature. I. Title.
  GV939.F29D69 2009
  796.33092—dc22
  [B]
                                                                2008041288

Every effort has been made to trace the owners of copyrighted material.
Lucent Books
27500 Drake Rd.
Farmington Hills, MI 48331

ISBN-13: 978-1-4205-0124-7
ISBN-10: 1-4205-0124-0

Printed in the United States of America
2 3 4 5 6 7 12 11 10

Printed by Bang Printing, Brainerd, MN, 2nd Ptg., 04/2010

Contents

F ame and celebrity are alluring. People are drawn to those who walk in fame's spotlight, whether they are known for great accomplishments or for notorious deeds. The lives of the famous pique public interest and attract attention, perhaps because their experiences seem in some ways so different from, yet in other ways so similar to, our own.

Newspapers, magazines, and television regularly capitalize on this fascination with celebrity by running profiles of famous people. For example, television programs such as *Entertainment Tonight* devote all of their programming to stories about entertainment and entertainers. Magazines such as *People* fill their pages with stories of the private lives of famous people. Even newspapers, newsmagazines, and television news frequently delve into the lives of well-known personalities. Despite the number of articles and programs, few provide more than a superficial glimpse at their subjects.

Lucent's People in the News series offers young readers a deeper look into the lives of today's newsmakers, the influences that have shaped them, and the impact they have had in their fields of endeavor and on other people's lives. The subjects of the series hail from many disciplines and walks of life. They include authors, musicians, athletes, political leaders, entertainers, entrepreneurs, and others who have made a mark on modern life and who, in many cases, will continue to do so for years to come.

These biographies are more than factual chronicles. Each book emphasizes the contributions, accomplishments, or deeds that have brought fame or notoriety to the individual and shows how that person has influenced modern life. Authors portray their subjects in a realistic, unsentimental light. For example, Bill Gates—the cofounder and chief executive officer of the software giant Microsoft—has been instrumental in making personal computers the most vital tool of the modern age. Few dispute his business savvy, his perseverance, or his technical expertise, yet critics say he is ruthless in his dealings with competitors and driven more by his desire to maintain Microsoft's dominance in the computer industry than by an interest in furthering technology.

In these books, young readers will encounter inspiring stories about real people who achieved success despite enormous obstacles. Oprah Winfrey—the most powerful, most watched, and wealthiest woman on television today—spent the first six years of her life in the care of her grandparents while her unwed mother sought work and a better life elsewhere. Her adolescence was colored by promiscuity, pregnancy at age fourteen, rape, and sexual abuse.

Each author documents and supports his or her work with an array of primary and secondary source quotations taken from diaries, letters, speeches, and interviews. All quotes are footnoted to show readers exactly how and where biographers derive their information and provide guidance for further research. The quotations enliven the text by giving readers eyewitness views of the life and accomplishments of each person covered in the People in the News series.

In addition, each book in the series includes photographs, annotated bibliographies, timelines, and comprehensive indexes. For both the casual reader and the student researcher, the People in the News series offers insight into the lives of today's newsmakers—people who shape the way we live, work, and play in the modern age.

The One and Only

Brett Favre's records and accomplishments on the football field are surpassed only by the heart with which he plays the game. At the end of the 2007 season, he held National Football League (NFL) records for touchdown passes (442), pass completions (5,377), passing yards (61,655 yards or 56,377m), and wins as a starting quarterback (160). He had started 253 consecutive regular-season games and played every one of them with an enthusiasm that made him look like a kid having a great time playing with his friends.

Favre won a Super Bowl and three Most Valuable Player (MVP) awards over his Green Bay Packers career, but perhaps his most awe-inspiring attribute has been his durability. Nothing kept him from starting a football game. He has played through numerous injuries and family tragedies. He admitted to drug abuse and a drinking problem, went into rehab, and emerged stronger than ever. No other player has his desire, grit, ability, heart, and unshakable ability to get out and play at game time.

There is no question that Favre is a superstar on the football field. He has earned the respect of his teammates and opponents by taking chances and making risky plays. He has been a competitor always focused on doing what he had to do to win ballgames. Yet Favre has been far from an untouchable football icon.

Favre's life has been studded with personal problems that often became the focus of public attention. He admitted that he needed help with an addiction to prescription painkillers, and he conceded that

Brett Favre, left, has been a respected leader both on and off the field. He is also a prankster with a penchant for practical jokes.

he needed to stop drinking alcohol because it was hurting his family life. His sorrow was apparent as he grieved the loss of his father, and he and his wife, Deanna, spoke openly about her battle with breast cancer. Favre's struggles off the field, matched with his enthusiasm at game time, made him human and endeared him to fans.

With his teammates, Favre has been both a respected leader and a prankster with a penchant for practical jokes. He might put something gooey into a teammate's shirt to make him start to sweat, but he is also prepared to do everything he can to give the team a chance at winning on game day. At game time, he is always excited to play and compete. That has long been clear by the way he reacts to touchdowns. He might lift his hands in the air, hug his teammates or even hoist them onto his shoulders and twirl them in the air. He cannot hide his exuberance when plays turn out as he hoped.

Favre is also a man with heart, reaching out to others in need. When a hurricane devastated his home state of Mississippi, he made sure donations of supplies made it through. He donates to children's charities in Mississippi and Wisconsin, providing disabled children with a playground that meets their needs and helping a horseback riding stable for disabled people keep going. He also understands how much it means for children to meet him, and he sets aside time to fulfill sick children's wishes through the Make-A-Wish Foundation. In addition, he learned from his mother, a special-education teacher, the importance of treating mentally disabled people with respect, and he has taken special care to include them in conversation and make them feel important throughout his life.

Favre has no trouble displaying a kind and easygoing nature off the field, but on the field his competitive side takes over. He has been blessed with amazing athletic ability, most notably a powerful right arm. On game day he is a gunslinger, using that arm with reckless abandon to do whatever he can to give his team a chance at winning. His focus on reaching the end zone sometimes results in costly mistakes, making him the NFL's leader in interceptions as well as touchdowns. He never lets those mistakes keep him from coming back and giving it another try, however, as his drive to compete compels him to continue playing to win.

When Favre left the Green Bay Packers for the New York Jets in 2008, he had broken every significant quarterback record in the books. His career has not been about records, however; it has been about competing and doing his best to win football games. Throughout his career he has been a reliable starter who always looks to score, and he has not lost touch with who he truly is: a quarterback from Kiln, Mississippi, who just loves to play the game.

Chapter One

A Natural Competitor

Sports have been a part of Brett Lorenzo Favre's life from the time he was born on October 10, 1969, in Gulfport, Mississippi. Brett, who grew up in nearby Kiln, Mississippi, was born on a fall Friday, a game day for his dad, Irv, who was a high school football coach. Brett arrived in time to allow his father to make it to the game, which, ironically, was against the Hancock North Central Hawks, the team Brett would later play for during high school.

Irv Favre took the assistant football coaching job at Hancock North Central High School in 1971 and eventually became the school's head football and baseball coach. He taught physical education and driver's education at the school, which housed students in grades one through twelve, and his wife, Bonita, was a special-education teacher there.

Irv Favre was a tough man. He had played baseball in college, and he passed a love of sports on to his children. Brett's brother Scott is three years older than he is, and his brother Jeff is four years younger. Their sister, Brandi, is seven years younger than Brett. While Brandi did not become a high school football quarterback like her brothers she did become a cheerleader and was eventually named Miss Teen Mississippi.

Scott, Brett, and Jeff showed an early interest in the game of football, and their parents encouraged them. Brett got his first football uniform at age three, and his mother would dress her children in little mascot uniforms and take them to their dad's

A young Brett (standing) eats po' boys at home with his family, (left to right) brother Scott, sister Brandi, his grandmother Izella French, mother Bonita, and father Big Irv.

games. Before long Brett was tagging along with his dad to football and baseball practices. Brett admired the high school players his father coached and aspired to be just like them.

A Good Life on Rotten Bayou

Brett grew up in Kiln (pronounced "kill"), a tiny town Brett describes as "a yellow caution light surrounded by a few businesses." The Favre family lived on Irvin Farve Road. Although the family's name was spelled wrong on the street sign, no one worried about fixing it. "Why?" Brett says. "It wouldn't change anything. Everybody knows my family lives down there."[1]

The Favre home rested on 50 acres (20ha) of land on Rotten Bayou, 12 miles (19km) from the Gulf of Mexico. The back deck of their home was practically on top of the waters of the bayou, and while Brett was growing up the family lost four dogs to the alligators that lived in the swamp. The occasional intruders were not a source of terror for the family, though, as the family was used to the snakes and alligators that came with living on the bayou.

Living close to Brett's family were Brett's grandmother, Izella French, whom he called Mee-Maw, and his aunt, Karen (Kay-Kay) Favre. Other neighbors were far away, however, so Brett grew up playing sports and getting into trouble with his brothers. A favorite game was called "Goal Line." One of the brothers would try to score against the other two, and the brother trying to score would get beaten unmercifully.

Brett and his brothers had their share of excitement and trouble. As a toddler, Brett had to have his stomach pumped out after he swallowed prescription medication. Another time, he toddled into

the bayou. When he was about eight years old, he and his brother Scott angered their dad by feeding cookies to the alligators that lived in the swamp. Irv Favre had to scare the gators away with a shotgun blast as the creatures headed toward the house.

The boys' games sometimes ended painfully. One time Brett shot Scott in the face with a BB gun. Another day, during a game of football, Brett threw a pass that Scott tried to catch, but he ended up falling into a glass window of the house. "We always seemed to get into trouble together," Brett said. "It's a wonder neither of us got killed."[2]

Brett played quarterback for Hancock North Central High School in 1986. His father Irv was his coach.

Playing with the Big Boys

Brett also spent a great deal of time with his father at the football and baseball practices for his dad's teams. He was in awe of the older players, but before long he realized that he also had a gift for athletics. When he was in grade school, he could throw a football as far as a high school quarterback. "I knew I had something special that other kids didn't," Brett says. "I used to dream that my arm would take me somewhere special some day."[3]

As a fifth-grader, Brett played his first organized football game. He started as a receiver, but after getting the wind knocked out of him, he told his coach he would rather play quarterback. He was moved to that position and scored three touchdowns. The cheers that he heard when the team scored made him decide that he wanted to play quarterback for a long time.

Even as a fifth-grader, his dad saw that Brett had the aggression and desire needed to be a successful athlete. "Brett heard it from me coaching," Irv Favre recalled. "You could go out and say it was just a game, that second place was OK sometimes, but that's not really true. You don't go out there to come in second. Heck, you go out there to win."[4]

Tough Love

When Brett got into Hancock North Central High School and joined the football team, his father became his coach. Irv Favre was a strict leader who stressed toughness, and he told his players not to try to win sympathy from him by pretending to be hurt. Brett took his words to heart. "Sometimes you get hit hard, and sometimes you don't feel like getting back up, but I always have, on and off the field,"[5] Brett says.

Irv Favre did not go easy on his son, and he expected him to be in top physical shape. Brett appreciated his father's attitude and spent nights working out, doing sit-ups and push-ups and lifting weights. Even on Friday nights after games he would work out. It was not his physical makeup that impressed his dad, however. "He had skill and he was big for his age, but not exceptional," his father remembered. "But I could tell that his being competitive could make the difference."[6]

A Sporty Romance

Sports was such a part of Brett Favre's life that it was even woven into his romance with his girlfriend, Deanna Tynes. One of Brett's gifts to her was a catcher's mitt and a mask so he could pitch to her. Brett was a pitcher with a powerful right arm, but Deanna was determined to prove that she could catch whatever he threw her way. Even when he fired the fastballs at her—and Brett's dad insisted that he was throwing too hard—she caught the ball. "My hand was on fire," she says, "but I wasn't about to tell him that."

Deanna Favre, *Don't Bet Against Me! Beating the Odds Against Breast Cancer and in Life.* Carol Stream, IL: Tyndale House, 2007, p. 17.

Brett did have a strong arm in high school, and he often threw the ball so hard that his receivers had trouble catching his passes. In practice, his powerful, wild throws would bounce off his receivers' chests and helmets. He did not have many opportunities to show off his arm strength in games, though, as Irv Favre ran an offense that stressed running plays rather than passing plays. Brett did not go against his father's game plan, and he sometimes ran with the ball himself.

Brett realized how much he loved football when he came down with mononucleosis as a high school sophomore. He could not play that season, and he missed the game terribly. He kept working out, however, and added muscle to his slim frame. His desire to get back to football also grew. "By the time I was a junior I was so anxious to play I felt like a little kid,"[7] he says.

High School Sweetheart

Brett loved sports, but while he was in high school his heart was pulled in another direction as well. When he was a freshman, he began dating sophomore Deanna Tynes. They had known each other since they had been young children, but they did not start thinking of each other as a boyfriend or girlfriend until a certain birthday party for Brett's older brother.

Bonita Favre had invited the members of the boys' and girls' basketball teams to the party, and Deanna was one of the guests. After a while Deanna went outside to shoot baskets in the driveway, and Brett watched her from inside the house for a time before summoning the courage to go talk to her. They played some one-on-one, and he tried to impress her by dunking the ball. While they felt awkward about being around one another, it helped that they were both good at sports. Soon after the party, Brett asked Deanna to be his girlfriend, and the pair dated throughout high school.

Making It into Southern Miss

Brett shared his dreams with Deanna, and one of those dreams was playing college football. The 6-foot-2 (1.8m, 5cm) 190-pound (86kg) quarterback was a strong, determined, and talented athlete, who played safety and punted in addition to quarterbacking his

Brett (4) avoids a tackle in a 1990 game against Georgia. Favre opted to attend Southern Mississippi because it was the only school that recruited him to play quarterback.

team to winning records his junior and senior seasons. He was talented enough to be chosen to play safety in the Mississippi High School All-Star Game, but his strong arm was somewhat of a secret because of the type of offense Irv Favre ran. The Hancock team used offenses that relied on the run more than the pass for yardage, and Brett threw for only 460 yards (421m) his senior season and about 800 (732m) during his entire high school career.

Bigger Is Not Always Better

Attending a low-profile school is not usually the first choice for a college athlete, but Brett Favre credits his choice of Southern Mississippi with giving him the experience he needed to make it to the pros. Favre, who started his first NFL game at age twenty-two, noted that if he had gone to a larger college, he probably would not have had the chance to play until he was a junior or a senior.

In 1999, after winning his third MVP award, Favre stated:

The advice I give to young players is this: don't give too much credence to the aura of the school; go where you will play. Southern Mississippi obviously isn't Quarterback U, and it's not going to contend for a championship any time soon. But look where I am today. I've accomplished a lot more than a lot of guys at those big schools ever will accomplish simply because I appreciated how hard it was to win ballgames and I was able to play every year.

Some guys only play one year of college football. They might have a great year, but they still don't know all of what is involved in a passing offense. They haven't seen enough. When I left college for the NFL I was 20 years old. I had played four college seasons and I didn't redshirt [refrain from playing in varsity games for a year to extend eligibility].

Brett Favre, *MVP*. Hallendale, FL: EGI, 2004, p. 15.

Recruiting letters from schools such as Auburn, Alabama, and Mississippi State arrived for Brett, but the only school that showed real interest in giving him a shot to play quarterback was Southern Mississippi. Irv Favre was in touch with the team's offensive line coach, and after the coach saw Brett heave the football 65 yards (59m), he promised him a scholarship if one became available.

No scholarships were open when it came time for Brett to decide on a school, however. Playing quarterback topped Brett's list of priorities when it came to choosing a college, so he decided to go to Pearl River Junior College in Poplarville, Mississippi. His girlfriend, Deanna, went to school there, and he hoped he would be offered the chance to play at a four-year school after his quarterbacking days at the two-year school came to an end. However, three days after he decided on Pearl River, he got a phone call from Southern Mississippi. Another player had decided not to play that season, and he was offered the last scholarship the school had. Brett was more than happy to change his plans and attend college at Southern Miss.

From Seventh String to Starter

When Favre arrived for football practice at Southern Mississippi in 1987, there were six quarterbacks ahead of him on the player roster. His lowly status did not faze the seventeen-year-old. "At least I'd get a chance to show them coaches what I could do at quarterback," he recalls. "That was all I ever asked for to begin with."[8]

Favre moved up rapidly. A few players got hurt, and one quarterback switched to receiver. By the time the season started, Favre was the third-string quarterback.

He sat on the bench during Southern Mississippi's first game of his freshman year, a 38–6 loss to Alabama. In the second game, Southern Miss fell behind to Tulane. Because the team's first- and second-string quarterbacks were not making any progress, the coach called for Favre to go into the game. The young quarterback had not expected to play, and he felt his stomach lurch.

With his team down 17–3, Favre ran to the huddle and looked into the eyes of his twenty-one- and twenty-two-year-old teammates. He was young and inexperienced, but his fellow players encouraged him. He had earned their friendship and respect in the few months he had been at Southern Miss, and they supported him as he prepared to take his first snaps as a college quarterback.

Favre did not let them down. He drove the team down the field, and as the team neared the end zone, Favre saw an open receiver and lobbed the ball to him. When the receiver caught the ball for a touchdown, Favre could not suppress his joy. He was so excited that he jumped on his coach and gave him a hug, and the team rallied to win 31–24. "When Brett threw his first touchdown pass, it reminded me of the peewee player he used to be," his mother recalls. "He was running around, jumping up and down, and hugging the coaches and players."[9]

Favre was the team's starter after the Tulane game, but he had an up-and-down freshman season. He threw four interceptions against Florida State, but he passed for five touchdowns and 527 yards (482m) in the final two games of the season. The Southern Mississippi Golden Eagles finished the season at 6–5. Favre had thrown for 1,264 yards (1,156m) and fifteen touchdowns as a freshman.

Unexpected Responsibility

After a successful freshman season, Favre was looking forward to his sophomore year as the team's quarterback. However, personal issues also weighed on his mind. His girlfriend, Deanna Tynes, was pregnant. He was eighteen and she was nineteen, and they were going to be parents. "We reacted like any young couple. We were scared,"[10] he says.

His parents offered to help financially and with the care of the child, and Favre felt reassured that he could stay in college and continue to play football. Favre had a successful season, throwing sixteen touchdowns with only five interceptions. He threw for 2,271 yards (2,077m), a new school record, and led his team to a 9–2 regular season record and a win over the University of Texas, El Paso, in the Independence Bowl. The game marked the first time Favre played on national television.

Favre's daughter, Brittany Nicole, was born on February 6, 1989. The Southern Mississippi coaching staff tried to keep the news quiet, but that did not keep the story from reaching the lo-

Brett relaxes at home with his wife, Deanna and his first daughter Brittany, who was born in 1989.

cal papers. Irv and Bonita Favre were too excited about their granddaughter to keep the news to themselves.

After Brittany's birth, Tynes graduated from the two-year-college she had been attending. She began working and took over most of the parenting duties while Favre continued his college career.

Favre for the Heisman

As Favre's junior year began, the media relations staff at Southern Mississippi campaigned to get Favre recognized as a candidate for the Heisman Trophy, an award given to the best college football player. The staff saw Favre's successful sophomore season as an opportunity to get people excited about their quarterback and school. Favre was not thrilled with the extra attention

In 1989 Favre led Southern Mississippi to a 30–26 victory over sixth-ranked Florida State and a top twenty ranking for his Golden Eagles.

that came with talk of the award, but he proved that he was deserving of it when he led his team to a 30–26 win over Florida State in the first game of the season. Florida State had been ranked as the sixth-best team in the nation, and after its win Southern Miss was in the top twenty for the first time since 1981.

The rest of the season did not go as well for Favre and the Golden Eagles. Favre threw for 2,563 yards (2,344m) and fourteen touchdowns that season, but the team lost three games in a row after the Florida State win and finished with a 5–6 record. The elation and attention that had come with the win over Florida State quickly evaporated.

Accident and Recovery

A car accident the following summer almost curtailed Favre's football career. On July 14, six weeks before the home opener at Southern

Miss, he was returning home after a day of fishing when his car hit a patch of gravel while traveling 70 miles (113km) per hour. The car flipped three times before hitting a pine tree. His brother, who had been following in another car, thought Favre had surely been killed.

Favre was knocked unconscious by the crash and was severely injured, but he was alive. On the way to the hospital, Favre worried that he would never play football again. He had hurt his back, liver, and abdomen and spent three days in intensive care. He went home after five days in the hospital, but three weeks later he began having severe stomach cramps. Doctors discovered that 30 inches (76cm) of his intestine had died. The intestine was removed, and in six weeks Favre lost 34 pounds (15kg). Doctors said he would not play football that year, but Favre was not so sure.

Number 4 Is a Fit for Favre

From fifth grade through high school, Brett Favre wore the number 10. He wanted to wear that number in college, but when he got to the University of Southern Mississippi, he was told that the number was not available. The number had belonged to quarterback Reggie Collier, and the school expected to retire it.

Favre's second choice for a number was 12. That was the number of his childhood heroes Roger Staubach and Terry Bradshaw. That number was already taken, however. Eleven, his brother Scott's number, was also unavailable.

Favre found to his chagrin that the only number left was 4. He took it reluctantly, but soon found that it fit him perfectly. He was one of the few players wearing the number, and Southern Mississippi used it in a slogan that promoted Favre for the Heisman Trophy, "'Favre 4 Heisman,'" he recalled. "I didn't win, but I loved the slogan."

Brett Favre and Chris Havel, *Favre: For the Record.* New York: Doubleday, 1997, p. 92.

Late that summer Favre returned to the practice field at Southern Mississippi, and his drive to play was unshakable. He begged his coach to let him play in the second game of the year, a game at Alabama. After being assured that Favre was strong enough, his coach agreed and decided to surprise his opponent. The team kept Favre's condition quiet all week, and Favre came in on the second play of the game.

Favre was sacked, but he rebounded and managed to connect on nine of seventeen passes for 125 yards (114m). He did not have a stellar game, but the Golden Eagles won 27–24. Coach Curley Hallman said Favre brought more to that game than physical ability: "Just his presence under the center was a big plus for our team."[11]

The team finished the season 8–3, including a 13–12 comeback victory over powerful Auburn, and it was invited to the All-American Bowl. During his college career, Favre displayed some of the attributes that would serve him well in the pros. "He'd see things around him," Hallman recalled. "He'd feel things he couldn't even see. I have been around guys who had the intensity in them, and they all were excellent players, but they just didn't have all the other things to go with it."[12]

A Family of Fans

Supporting Favre at every home college football game was his personal cheering section. His parents, cousins, aunts, and uncles would show up at games wearing matching black and gold T-shirts identifying themselves as "Brett Favre's Mom" or "Brett Favre's Aunt." "The other Golden Eagles fans couldn't wait to see what we were wearing when we arrived at the tailgates," Bonita Favre says. "I'm sure Brett was probably embarrassed when the Favre Clan made their grand appearance, but we had fun!"

Brett Favre and Bonita Favre, *Favre*. New York: Rugged Land, 2004, p. 200.

Turning Pro

Favre finished his college career at Southern Mississippi with school records for yards gained and touchdowns scored. He prepared for the NFL draft and expected to be chosen. But Favre was not considered one of the top picks. He had been a great athlete from the time he was a child, but he was not tagged as a superstar.

Favre had seen plenty of game action and had a strong college football career, but Southern Mississippi was a low-profile school. He had only been on national television four times in his college career, and the car accident before his senior season hampered his strength. Some pro football coaches and scouts showed enough interest in him to take a look at what he could do, however, and he now waited to see what the rest of his football career would bring.

Chapter Two

Struggles and Superstardom

With his college football days behind him, Favre now awaited draft day to learn the fate of his football future. He had no expectations of greatness or thoughts of glory. He was simply looking forward to getting into the NFL, and he hoped to have a chance to play. The Atlanta Falcons had shown the most interest in him before the draft, and that was the team he expected to join.

Favre hoped to be one of the first fifteen players chosen on draft day, but as April 21, 1991, wore on, his name was not mentioned in the initial draft picks. Favre was not alone as he waited; a hundred family members and friends gathered around him at the Favre home in Mississippi to await word on his future. Many family members wore draft day T-shirts they had made for the occasion. The tension grew as the first round passed without a call to Favre, and he became irritated that he was not being chosen. "With every pick, the agony grew longer and stronger," Bonita Favre says. "After the first round, it really got agonizing."[13]

An excited Favre talks to the Atlanta Falcons after they picked him in the second round of the NFL draft.

Finally, the Falcons took Favre with the thirty-third pick of the draft. A relieved Favre was happy it was over. Around him, pandemonium broke out. "Everyone was jumping up and down, screaming and hollering congratulations," Bonita recalls. "In this part of the world, it was like Mardi Gras."[14]

Frustration with the Falcons

Favre was happy to begin life as a professional football player in Atlanta. He expected to enjoy his job, and he threw two touchdown passes in preseason games. Once the season started,

Favre stands for a photo with Falcons' coach Jerry Glanville after signing with the Falcons. Their relationship was strained and in 1992 Favre was traded to the Green Bay Packers.

however, he was relegated to the third-string quarterback position, behind Chris Miller and Billy Joe Tolliver. He bided his time there, going to practice during the day and heading out for some beers at night with friends.

It did not help Favre's situation that he did not get along well with the team's brash coach, Jerry Glanville. When Favre overslept, got caught in traffic, and was late for the team picture, he ran into Glanville just as the coach was pulling out of the parking lot. Favre was fined fifteen hundred dollars for missing the photo. Before one game Glanville teased Favre about his lack of playing time and proceeded to tell him there would have to be a string of disasters before Favre would get a shot at playing. Favre did make it into two games and threw five passes before the 1991 season came to a close.

Bad Hip?

The Green Bay Packers traded for Favre in 1992, but he almost did not pass the team's physical examination. During the inspection, doctors discovered Favre had a bad hip. In his autobiography, Favre says he injured the hip in the East-West Shrine game in his senior year of college. The doctors suggested that Favre be let go.

General manager Ron Wolf allowed Favre to play even though the doctors only expected Favre to last three or four years in the league. Wolf dismissed their reservations and stuck with Favre. "They wanted to send him back," Wolf says. "They were incorrect in their assessment."

Mike Spofford, "Some Untold Favre Stories," Packers.com, March 3, 2008. www. packers. com.

A Surprise Move

Given his lack of playing time and strained relationship with the coach, it would have been easy for Favre to let himself think that the Falcons viewed him as expendable. However, he expected to stay with the team, and he thought that it would simply take time for him to get his chance to show what he could do. When he got a call in February 1992 from the Green Bay Packers' general manager, Ron Wolf, Favre was stunned. The Packers had traded a first-round draft pick to the Falcons, and they were bringing Favre to Green Bay. Wolf reassured him that the Packers wanted him badly and that in Green Bay he would have a chance to contend for more playing time.

Favre did not know where Green Bay was, and once he made it to the city in northeast Wisconsin, Packers fans were not sure for whom their team had just traded a first-round pick. People had trouble pronouncing his name, but the strong arm he showed in training camp began to win the fans over. Coach Mike Holmgren, who was also spending his first season in Green Bay, agreed with Wolf's assessment. "When you get a chance to get a quarter-back that you think is a great one, you do it,"[15] he says.

Striking Gold in Green Bay

The Packers had gone 4–12 in the 1991 season with quarterback Don Majkowski, and Wolf brought in Holmgren and Favre with hopes of turning things around. Favre was not too concerned about buckling down and learning Holmgren's complex offensive system too quickly, however. He had been a backup quarterback in Atlanta and assumed he would have the same role in Green Bay. "I felt like in time, I would get a chance to play, but [Majkowski] was smooth in the huddle," Favre says. "He was the starter. I didn't see that changing, at least not early in the 1992 season."[16]

Majkowski started the first three games that season, but in the third game, against the Cincinnati Bengals, Majkowski was sacked. He tore ligaments in his ankle and had to leave the game. Favre's stomach buckled as he nervously put on his helmet and ran onto the field.

Favre's first plays as the Packers' quarterback were not things of beauty. He struggled, and fans chanted for backup Ty Detmer to take over. "I made enough mistakes in this first half to last the

Early in his career with the Packers, Favre's playing was inconsistent but he executed plays when it counted.

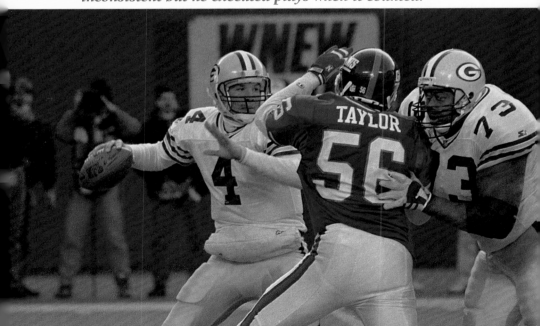

whole year," he said after the game, "and I was wondering if they were going to run me out of town."[17]

Favre executed when it counted, however. With about a minute left in the game, the Packers were behind 23–17. They were on their own 8 yard (7.3m) line, 92 yards (84m) away from the end zone, and had no time-outs. On the fifth play of the drive, Favre found Kitrick Taylor, threw a 35-yard (32m) pass, and closed his eyes. "I couldn't bear to look," he says. "I just closed my eyes and waited for the crowd to let me know."[18] The cheers soon told him that Taylor had scored, and the Packers won 24–23. Favre was so happy that he head-butted 300-pound (136kg) guard Ron Hallstrom. His forehead started bleeding, but he was too excited to feel it. "I played pretty wild but found a way to get it done," he says. "I knew there was no way I was going to sit on the bench again. I had too much fun that day."[19]

Playing in Pain

Favre was the Packers' starter after that game, and in his seventh start of the season he displayed the toughness that would become one of his defining characteristics. In a game against the Philadelphia Eagles on November 15, he was sacked by All-Pro defensive end Reggie White. Favre's shoulder was separated, but he feared he would lose his starting spot if he asked to sit out. He opted to have doctors give him a shot of Novocain to take away the pain. It worked, and Favre led the Packers to a 27–24 win.

Favre's play was uneven that first year, but he helped the team turn things around. The Packers finished the season with a 9–7 record, and they just missed making the playoffs. Favre threw three interceptions in the last game of the season, a 27–7 loss to the Minnesota Vikings that kept the team out of the playoffs. However, his contributions to the team were noted and he was named to the Pro Bowl.

Young Gun

Favre's determination to play while injured in the game against Philadelphia made the Packers a stronger team the next season. Favre's

A Rocky Beginning

Favre did not have a quiet transition to life as a Green Bay Packer. He quickly made friends with his teammates, and the twenty-two-year-old enjoyed going out with his buddies. After the team's summer minicamp in 1992, he returned to the south with some friends from the team, got into a bar fight, and was arrested. He sat in jail for a few hours until his agent bailed him out.

Worse than the legal punishment for his crime was the publicity his arrest received and the reaction he got from his coach. After the story made the national papers, Favre had an uncomfortable phone conversation with Mike Holmgren, who made it clear that he would not tolerate that kind of behavior from his players. Favre also nervously called Ron Wolf, expecting some repercussions for his actions. Wolf, however, simply told him that the next time he got in a fight, he should make sure he won.

toughness made such an impression on Reggie White that the iconic defensive player signed with the team before the 1993 season.

Favre's first full season as a starter was a struggle as he tried to master Holmgren's difficult offense and faced intense pressure from opposing defenses. The team played well, but Favre was inconsistent. After making a mistake, he would try to make a big play to make up for it. This would often result in an interception. He also had enthusiasm, competitiveness, and determination; these attributes brought an element of excitement to the game every time the ball was snapped.

In a comeback win against the New Orleans Saints on November 14, Favre showed he could be counted on in pressure situations. The Packers were at their own 27-yard (25m) line, facing second down with 20 yards (18m) to go. With fifty-two seconds in the game, Favre rolled out of the pocket, spotted receiver Sterling Sharpe, and hit him with a 54-yard (49m) pass to set up a game-winning field goal.

Favre gave fans another exciting finale against Tampa Bay on November 28. Although he suffered a deep thigh bruise in the game, he limped back onto the field and hit Sharpe with a 2-yard (1.8m) touchdown pass with only one minute and sixteen seconds left on the clock. The play capped a 75-yard (66m) scoring drive that gave the Packers a win.

The Packers finished the season 9–7 and made their first trip to the playoffs in eleven years. Facing the Detroit Lions in a National Football Conference (NFC) wild card playoff game, Favre again showed his ability to come through in pressure-filled situations. With the Packers behind 24–21 in the final minute of the game, he scrambled to his left, found Sharpe open, and tossed the ball across his body. The pass traveled about 70 yards (64m) across the field and into the receiver's hands. Sharpe scored, giving the Packers a 28–24 victory. The unconventional throw furthered Favre's image as a quarterback who could pull off unbelievable plays. It was clear that he had the knack for doing whatever it took to get his team a win. "It was the play of the year,"[20] Holmgren says.

The Packers lost the next week to Dallas in an NFC divisional playoff, but Favre's reputation had been sealed. He was chosen as a Pro Bowl reserve and ended the season first among NFC passers and second in the NFL with 318 completions.

Clashes with the Coach

The Packers gave Favre a four-year, $19 million contract extension the next season, and in 1994 he had amazing moments as well as terrible ones. He showed his best side in games like the September 25 contest at Tampa Bay, during which he threw for 306 yards (280m) and three touchdowns in a 30–3 win. However, he was also prone to throwing interceptions and still struggled with Holmgren's complex offense.

A stern and demanding coach, Holmgren was tough on Favre. He knew the quarterback had talent and wanted him to stop trying to force big plays. The team had gone 9–7 and had made the playoffs the previous season, and Favre thought that had been a

Packer coach Mike Holmgren, left, stuck with Favre despite inconsistent play long enough for Favre to understand the offense.

good year for the team. Holmgren wanted more: a Super Bowl win. "We had a test of wills," Holmgren says. "He's a knucklehead. His way was simply not going to be good enough."[21]

Favre's starting job was in jeopardy after he had to leave a game against Minnesota on October 20 because of a bruised left hip. It was the first time since becoming a starter in 1992 that he left a game due to injury. Backup Mark Brunell came into the game and did well, but the Packers lost 13–10 in overtime. After the game, Holmgren considered benching Favre. He had thrown forty-six touchdowns in thirty-eight games, but he had also thrown forty-four interceptions. The team's offensive coaches wanted to put Brunell into the starting job.

Holmgren, however, decided to stick with Favre. He thought that the quarterback was close to understanding the offense and that he could get him to stop forcing plays. "We're joined at the hip," Holmgren told Favre. "Either we're going to the Super Bowl together, or we're going down together."[22]

Stopped by Dallas

Favre showed that he could give the team a lift when it mattered when the Packers took on the Falcons on December 18. The Packers had to win in order to make it to the playoffs. With less than a minute in the game and no time-outs left, the Packers were behind 17–14. They had the ball at Atlanta's 9-yard (8.2m) line on third down, with one yard to go for a first down. Favre dropped back and looked toward the end zone but could not find an open receiver. Rather than throwing the ball away to stop the clock, he headed for the end zone himself. He landed just inside the goal line, and the Packers won 21–17. "The whole season was carrying on my shoulders," he says. "[Coach] Mike [Holmgren] said 'Did you know if you didn't get in, we might not have enough time left?' I said I never even thought of that. I knew I was going to get in from the five-yard [4.6m] line."[23]

The Packers went 9–7 again in 1994 and beat Detroit 16–12 in the NFC wild card game at Green Bay's Lambeau Field on December 31. They again met Dallas in the divisional playoff game and lost to the Cowboys. Favre and the Packers were close to making it to the Super Bowl but still were not quite good enough.

A Solid Foundation

Although Favre had not yet taken his team to the top of the NFL, his popularity was on the rise. As he became more well known, he had to deal with the reality of being a celebrity as well as an athlete. He was extremely popular in Green Bay and had to come to terms with being recognized wherever he went. This did not keep him at home, however, and he enjoyed going out with his friends and playing golf. He also found enjoyment in more solitary pursuits, however, such as hunting.

Favre's success also meant that he had to figure out how to deal with requests for assistance that came his way. Throughout his professional career he had set time aside to meet with sick children through the Make-A-Wish Foundation program, but he and his girlfriend (who later became his wife), Deanna Tynes, received many requests for aid from others as well. Favre and Tynes were not sure how to cope with requests from people who were ill or having financial difficulty. A friend suggested that they choose one cause to support. They easily decided to help special-needs children. Favre's mother taught special education, and he had always gotten along well with her students.

Favre's off-the-field interests include hunting. Here, he is seen hunting deer in Wisconsin in 1998.

Favre and Tynes established an annual celebrity softball game, golf tournament, and steak dinner to raise money for the Brett Favre Fourward Foundation. The organization began providing support to the Special Olympics and smaller programs that helped children with special needs. "What better investment than children?" Tynes asks. "We feel they're so important."[24]

Down Go the Champs

Off the field, Favre was learning how to cope with being a celebrity, and on the field he was becoming a more polished player. By 1995 Favre had a firmer understanding of Holmgren's offense and was clearly the team's leader. The Packers had an 11–5 record in 1995 and finished the season on top of the NFC Central Division. The Packers had shown they were a good team. Now they had to prove they were among the NFL's elite.

Favre threw three touchdowns as the Packers won the wild card game 37–20 over Atlanta at Lambeau Field on December 31. The team then faced San Francisco in the divisional playoff. The 49ers, the Super Bowl champions of the previous season, were heavily favored, but Favre was not nervous about facing them. The Packers were not supposed to win, so the twenty-six-year-old felt no pressure. Favre passed for two touchdowns, and the Packers beat the favored 49ers, 27–17. He completed twenty-one of twenty-eight passes for 299 yards (273m). Favre's big plays included a completion to tight end Keith Jackson, a pass made

Playing in Pain

Favre's reputation for toughness was proven in a game against the Chicago Bears on November 12, 2005. Favre had severely sprained his ankle against the Vikings a week earlier, and no one knew if he would be able to start against the Bears. He spent the week on crutches, but the durable Favre not only started the game, but he also threw for 336 yards (307.238m) and five touchdowns as the Packers won 35–28. With his ankle still bothering him against Cleveland on November 19, he passed for three touchdowns and ran for another one.

Favre's ability to bounce back from injury helped the Packers clinch the 2005 division title on December 24. In the game against the Pittsburgh Steelers, Favre scrambled and was hit by three defenders. The Packers called a time-out, and Favre went to the sideline and coughed up blood. He returned to the game and tossed a 1-yard (.9m) pass to Mark Chmura in the end zone on the next play. Although he had the wind knocked out of him twice in that game, he still threw for two touchdowns and 301 yards (275m). The Packers clinched their division with a 24–19 win.

Favre's teammates knew they could count on him to be in the game. "Brett's not coming out of the game unless a bone's sticking out," said backup quarterback Ty Detmer.

Peter King, "Bitter Pill," *Sports Illustrated*, May 27, 1996, p. 24.

as Favre was getting his balance back after slipping. He was showing the team what it took to be a winner. "We've said all along, if we're going to win it all, he's going to show us the way and he's showing us the way,"[25] said Mark Chmura, another tight end for the Packers.

More to Come

Once again, however, the Packers lost the NFC championship game to Dallas. On January 14, 1996, the Cowboys beat the Packers 38–27. Favre threw for 307 yards (281m), three touchdowns, and two interceptions. The Packers were close to being the best, but that achievement still eluded them.

It was clear, however, that Favre had found his niche in Green Bay. He was named the NFL's Most Valuable Player of 1995 and was chosen as a Pro Bowl starter. He and Holmgren went through some rough times as Favre struggled to learn the offense, but his athletic ability and refusal to give up in the face of injury kept him in the starting job and sowed the seeds of greatness to come.

Chapter Three

From Rehab to the Super Bowl

Favre had become a capable leader on the football field, earning the respect of his teammates with his powerful arm and competitive attitude. The 1995 season had been Favre's best in the NFL to date. He finished the season with 4,413 passing yards (4,035m) to top the league. In addition to Pro Bowl and Most Valuable Player (MVP) honors, he received the Pro Football Performer of the Year Award from ESPN. However, Favre also had a secret that he hid well. He had developed a serious addiction to painkillers.

Few knew that Favre was stumbling when it came to managing his personal life. Confrontations with his girlfriend, Deanna Tynes, and a scare after a postseason operation led him to finally admit to himself the depth of his problem. He initially thought he could beat the addiction on his own, but he was later convinced to get help. While he was fighting through this personal struggle, he continued to keep his mind on football and the Packers' quest for an NFL title.

Repercussions

Favre's addiction did not impact his play on the field, and he did not take the pills on the days leading up to game days. However, the Vicodin impacted his personal life and his physical well-being.

During the season Favre was living with his girlfriend and their daughter in a four-bedroom house not far from Lambeau Field.

The Beginnings of a Serious Problem

Favre's addiction to Vicodin worsened during the 1995 season. He had taken Vicodin at times early in his career to dull the pain after an injury or surgery, but his addiction had its roots in the team trip home from the 1993 season opener. The team had played the game in Milwaukee, at Milwaukee County Stadium, and Favre and some teammates took the pills as they rode the bus back to Green Bay.

For the rest of the 1993 season, Favre would borrow a few Vicodin pills from teammates who had been prescribed the pain medication. He did not take the pills in the off-season, but he began again the next year. On the weekends he stayed away from the pills, but by late in the 1994 season he felt he needed to have them regularly during the week.

Hernia surgery in early 1995 gave him access to Vicodin in that off-season, as he was prescribed the drug for pain. He complained of pain much longer than he actually had it and went from taking six pills a night to taking ten.

However, he would often choose to go out drinking with his friends rather than spend time with them. His drug addiction brought on mood swings and sleeplessness that were not helped by his drinking. When he was home, he was short-tempered. "He was loud, rough, and often hateful," Tynes, now Deanna Favre, said. "I saw the first signs of a mean streak I didn't know Brett had."[26]

Favre had a routine of taking the pills during the week at 9:00 P.M., and as his addiction wore on, he was taking as many as fifteen a night. He even took them when he was at the ESPY Awards ceremony, where he had been selected by ESPN as the Pro Football Performer of the Year. He spent twenty minutes trying to get all the pills down before the show.

Favre was sneaky about acquiring the painkillers, asking many players for a few pills to help him get past some aches and pains.

Because he was getting the pills from so many different sources, no one suspected the depth of his addiction. He was still playing well and would strongly deny being addicted if he was questioned about it. "What I didn't know was that he was using everyone he knew—me, the team doctors, his trainers, and his teammates—to get painkillers,"[27] Tynes says.

As the season wore on, she realized the severity of his addiction. He was not sleeping and would watch television or play solitaire on the computer for hours. He would throw up badly and became severely constipated. His family and close friends on the team, as well as quarterbacks coach Steve Mariucci, also began to suspect something. "We'd tell him time and again: 'You've got to cut this out.' But players think they're invincible, and Brett was no different,"[28] says Packers tight end Mark Chmura.

It was difficult for Tynes to get team doctors to realize how severe Favre's addiction had become, or to get him to realize what

President Bill Clinton talks to Favre in 1996 and offers his support in Brett's fight against addiction to painkiller drugs.

he was doing to himself. "I'd do anything to get [Vicodin]. Beg. Borrow. You name it. In the back of my mind I knew it was a pretty screwed up way to live but I didn't care," Favre says. "The next day I would tell myself how stupid it was to act like that, but a couple of hours later I'd start wanting the pills again."[29]

Admission

Favre's treatment of Tynes led her to threaten to leave him in early 1996. He stopped taking the pills that February out of concern for their relationship, and a routine operation later that month led him to get treatment for his addiction.

In late February, Favre had surgery to remove bone spurs in his ankle. Tynes and their daughter were with him in the hospital after the operation. As Favre was talking to them, his eyes rolled back into his head and his arms and legs began to shake. His daughter asked if he was going to die, and Tynes rushed her out of the room as doctors and nurses attended to Favre. After twenty minutes Favre was stabilized. Fearing the seizure was related to the pain pills he had been taking, he told the doctors how many he had been taking and for how long.

Favre's doctors promised to help him get rid of his addiction. After news of his addiction reached NFL officials, an NFL counselor recommended he enter a treatment center. Favre thought he could handle his recovery himself and was reluctant to go to rehab. However, NFL doctors and officials insisted. After being threatened with a hefty fine, and not wanting to jeopardize the Packers' coming season, he agreed to go. Favre entered the Menninger Clinic in Topeka, Kansas, in mid-May 1996 and spent seven weeks in treatment.

Treatment

The clinic resembles a college campus, and Favre spent his days there talking to counselors, meeting with others in rehab for group therapy, and spending time thinking about his life and attitude toward others. He talked about his addiction to the painkillers and also discussed his drinking. "I thought a lot about what was

Going Public

Favre speaks at a Packer press conference with a supportive Mike Holmgren by his side about his stay at the Menninger Clinic in the drug rehabilitation program.

Before entering rehab, Favre faced the media and went public with news of his addiction. He knew it would not be an easy thing to do, but he felt it was best to get the news out in the open. It would be clear that something was going on when he did not report to the team's preseason mini-camp, and he wanted to be up front about his addiction and trip to rehab. Favre told the reporters that his addiction was a serious problem that he needed to take care of for the good of himself, his family, and his team.

The fact that he wanted to face the media did not make it any easier, however. "I started talking and my leg started shaking something awful," he says. "The next thing you know, I'm standing there telling them my life story. That was the hardest part of all. It was a pretty humbling experience, to say the least."

Brett Favre and Chris Havel, *Favre: For the Record.* New York: Doubleday, 1997, p. 48.

good and bad in my life," he says. "And about what I could do to be a better person. It was the first time I ever actually sat back and thought about it."[30]

Not everything at the center went well. Favre thought he should have the freedom to leave the clinic. When he was denied a weekend pass to see Tynes, he became so infuriated he punched a hole in a wall. He struggled with the fact that he needed to stay at the clinic to complete his treatment.

While he was there, he did not forget about his commitment to his team. He used his time to get into great physical shape. He ate plenty of fruits and vegetables and chose to drink water over soda. He worked out and made his body stronger. He was not practicing with his team or studying the playbook, but he was getting his body ready for the next season.

Favre eventually came to see that his stay at the treatment center was the best thing for him at the time. He did need help to get over his addiction, and he got it at the clinic. "I found out trying to deal with drug addiction by myself leads to rock bottom," he says. "It leads to losing your family, your job, and your life."[31]

Favre left the Menninger Clinic in the summer of 1996 and took a new look at his life. The NFL required him to give up alcohol for a time, and he stopped drinking. He realized how poorly he had been treating the people who were closest to him. He asked Tynes to marry him, several times, and eventually she agreed. They were married in a small ceremony at St. Agnes Catholic Church in Green Bay on July 14, 1996.

At the press conference following his release from rehab, Favre stressed that he wanted to look at the team's future rather than dwell on his past problems. With the help of the staff at the clinic, he had overcome his dependency on prescription painkillers. He

Brett and Deanna were married on July 14, 1996.

was looking forward to what he and the Packers could accomplish. "All I can tell people is if you don't believe me, bet against me because eventually they'll lose," he said at the time. "I'm going to beat this thing. I'm going to the Super Bowl."[32]

On Their Way

Favre erased any doubts people might have had about him in the first game of the 1996 season. On September 1 he threw four touchdowns against the Tampa Bay Buccaneers in a game the Packers won 34–3. It was his first of five season games in which he threw four touchdowns.

One of his most spectacular plays that season was a 50-yard (46m) Hail Mary pass to wide receiver Antonio Freeman. It came on the last play of the first half at Chicago on October 6, in a game the Packers won 37–6. Another impressive Packer win came in

Fourward

In 1996 Favre established the Brett Favre Fourward Foundation. It provides aid to disadvantaged children in Wisconsin and Mississippi and has given more than $1.5 million to charities. Among the dozens of charities the foundation supports in Mississippi are the Salvation Army, the Special Olympics, the Association for Retarded Citizens, and the Make-A-Wish Foundation. In Wisconsin, the foundation supports the Make-A-Wish Foundation, United Cerebral Palsy of Wisconsin, and the Special Olympics, among others.

Favre was a baseball player while in high school, so it made sense that he and his wife, Deanna, would raise money for the foundation through a ballgame. Favre sponsored an annual celebrity softball game in Wisconsin to raise money for the foundation. In Mississippi, he staged an annual celebrity golf tournament to raise money. In 2005 he and his wife also founded the Deanna Favre Hope Foundation to help underinsured and uninsured breast cancer patients.

a Monday Night Football game on October 14 against the San Francisco 49ers. Favre led the team on three scoring drives in the second half, including a 59-yard (54m) touchdown pass to wide receiver Don Beebe. The Packers kicked one field goal in the fourth quarter to tie and another in overtime to win 23–20.

Favre was an important part of the Packers juggernaut as the team raced to a 13–3 record. The team won its second straight division title, scoring more points on offense than any team in the league and giving Green Bay a taste of the glory it had not experienced since the 1960s under legendary coach Vince Lombardi. The Packers had other standout players, including defensive end Reggie White, safety LeRoy Butler, defensive lineman Gilbert Brown, tight ends Mark Chmura and Keith Jackson, and punt returner Desmond Howard, but Favre was the team's leader. He won his second straight MVP that year, and he was chosen as the Pro Football Performer of the Year by ESPN's ESPY Awards. For the second year in a row, he led the NFL in touchdown passes and set a conference record with thirty-nine touchdown passes. "When he runs onto the field, the field automatically tilts in your favor," says Ron Wolf, the Packers' general manager. "He's highly competitive. There's still a fire burning in his belly. He wants to achieve. He wants to win. More importantly, he likes to play the game."[33]

Finally, the Super Bowl

The Packers seemed destined to make it to the Super Bowl that year. They faced the San Francisco 49ers at Lambeau Field on a cold, rainy January 4, 1997, with the temperature hovering just above freezing. Favre had a difficult time gripping the ball with his ice-cold hands, but he still managed to toss a 4-yard (3.7m) touchdown pass to wide receiver Andre Rison that put the team up 14–0. Thanks to a pair of long punt returns by Desmond Howard, including one for a touchdown, the Packers won 35–14.

Next up for the Packers at Lambeau Field were the Carolina Panthers. The temperature was a bone-chilling 3 degrees (-16°C) at kickoff time, and the wind whipping through the stadium made it feel like -17 degrees (-22°C). It was the coldest playoff game in Green Bay since the historic Ice Bowl, when the Packers beat the

Favre fires off a pass during the January 1997 NFC Championship game. Favre threw two touchdown passes in leading his team to the Super Bowl.

Dallas Cowboys with a last-minute quarterback sneak to win the NFL championship on December 31, 1967.

Favre had an easier time with the Panthers than Bart Starr had had with the Cowboys that day. He had a tough start to the game, throwing an interception to Sam Mills, in the first quarter, but he tossed a 29-yard (27m) touchdown pass to running back Dorsey Levens in the next quarter. He later fumbled the ball, but near the end of the first half found Antonio Freeman for a touchdown to cap a 71-yard (65m) drive. Levens ran for 205 yards (187m) that day, and the Packers won 30–13. Favre and the Packers were going to the Super Bowl, and Favre was excited to share the joy of the moment with the hometown fans who stayed to the end of the bitterly cold contest. "It was packed and people were enjoying it as much as we were, if not more. People were crying and excited," he says. "Standing on that podium and looking around was like, well, this is it. We have finally arrived. I said to myself, 'No one ever thought I'd be here this early, but here I am and I'm going to enjoy it.'"[34]

Super Team

Favre was anxious in the hours leading up to his Super Bowl debut. The Packers faced the New England Patriots at the Super Dome in New Orleans in Super Bowl XXXI on January 26, 1997. Favre hoped he would not be too nervous to perform at the level his teammates were expecting. Once he got onto the field, however, nerves soon gave way to exuberance. On his second snap of the game, Favre took a look at the defensive line facing him and could sense that New England was going to come at him hard. He felt a blitz coming his way. To take advantage of the situation, he improvised. He called a play that sent Andre Rison and Antonio Freeman to the left side of the field. Favre was counting on the Patriots not being able to cover Rison, and he was right. Rison zipped past his defender, and Favre found him at the 20-yard (18m) line with a 54-yard (49m) pass. Rison easily sauntered into the end zone, and Favre ripped off his helmet and took off across the field. He had thrown his first Super Bowl touchdown and could not hide his enthusiasm.

The Patriots came back to take a 14–10 lead, but they did not hold it for long. Favre saw Freeman get away from defender Lawyer Milloy and sent a pass to Freeman along the right sideline. Freeman took the pass into the end zone for an 81-yard (74m) touchdown, at that time the longest reception ever in Super Bowl history. Favre felt like he could not miss. "The Super Bowl was one of my most enjoyable games ever," he says. "I felt so clear and so at ease."[35]

Shortly before the half ended, Favre scored himself. He and the Packers made it to the Patriots' 2-yard (1.8m) line. Favre rolled out and intended to pass to Mark Chmura. Chmura was covered, however, so Favre kept the ball himself. He plunged toward the end zone and just managed to get the ball over the goal line before he rolled out of bounds. The Packers led 27–14 at halftime and went on to win 35–21 after a 99-yard (91m) kickoff return by game MVP Desmond Howard and a two-point conversion from Favre to Chmura.

After the game, reporters swarmed around Favre as his wife made her way through the crowd with their daughter. When

Favre celebrates throwing a touchdown pass in the first quarter of Super Bowl XXXI. The Packers would win their third Super Bowl title.

Deanna made it to his side, he gave her a hug and a kiss and held his daughter as he enjoyed the victory. "This means everything," he said at the time. "I've been through a lot of tough times this year and a lot of good. They both kind of equal themselves out, and you take the good with the bad. To win this is unbelievable."[36]

In a League of His Own

Favre wanted to do more than win games as a good quarterback. He wanted to be the best at what he did. In his 1997 autobiography, Favre indicates that he wanted to make his mark on the NFL. He wanted to play at a level that ensured he would not be forgotten. "My goal is to be the best of all time," he says, "and up to now I've had some pretty good luck in reaching that goal."[37] With a pair of MVP awards and a Super Bowl ring, he was clearly one of the NFL's greats.

Chapter Four

Disappointment and Frustration

Favre continued to make an impact on the NFL during the next season. He was again running the show for the Packers, and the pieces were in place for the team to make a repeat appearance in the Super Bowl. Reggie White, Gilbert Brown, and LeRoy Butler were there to lead the defense. Antonio Freeman and Robert Brooks were starting as receivers, and Dorsey Levens continued to run the ball. With Favre at quarterback, there was no doubt about the team's ability to put points on the board.

The team was on a roll, and Favre loved it. He never stopped striving to reach the end zone, taking chances in order to score. His risks often paid off, and it appeared that the team would roll through another championship season. Winning seemed to come so easily that Favre expected the team's success to last. However, it did not take long for him to learn that success is sometimes fleeting.

Record Breaker

Favre's strong arm consistently put points on the board during the 1997 through 1998 football season. In the fourth game of the season, he surpassed the Packers' team record for touchdowns. He threw touchdown pass number 153 against the Vikings on September 21, breaking a team record it had taken Bart Starr sixteen years to set. While the team's pass-centered style of play had something to do with Favre hitting the record much earlier in his career, there was also no doubt that he was making as much of an impact on his team and the NFL as the legendary Starr.

The Packers were also making their mark on the league. The team proved it deserved the title of NFL champions when the Packers faced the Patriots in a rematch on October 27. Favre threw for 239 yards (219m) and three touchdowns in the 28–10 win. In a showdown against the Cowboys on November 23, Favre and the Packers showed just how dominant they had become. The Cowboys had beaten the Packers eight times in a row, but this time the tide turned. Favre threw four touchdown passes, and the Packers won 45–17 at Lambeau Field. "It's great to finally beat

The Joker

Favre seriously wanted to win football games, but he also loved practical jokes. Once, on a cold winter day, he took teammate Frank Winters's car and drove it far away from the players' parking lot. He turned on the air conditioner and radio and then accidentally locked the keys in the car. A locksmith had to come over to the stadium to let Winters into his car.

During a 1998 preseason game, Favre got the best of quarterbacks coach Andy Reid. Reid gave Favre a play, looked away toward the field, and looked back to find Favre missing. Coach Mike Holmgren yelled at Reid to get Favre into the game, but Reid could not see him. The team took a penalty, and Reid turned to see Favre standing next to him, hiding behind his left side.

Favre's teammates and coaches were not the only ones who were at the receiving end of his practical jokes. After a production meeting with announcers from the Fox television network before the NFC championship game against the San Francisco 49ers in January 1998, Favre set off a stink bomb. "John Madden had some sort of adverse reaction," Favre says. "He was bracing himself against the wall, looking ill."

Quoted in *Sports Illustrated*, "Brett-Time Stories," March 12, 2008, p. 70.
Quoted in Michael Silver, "Second to None," *Sports Illustrated*, January 19, 1998, p. 30.

Favre holds high the NFC championship trophy after the Packers' 23–10 win over the San Francisco 49ers.

these guys; it's a shame it took so long," Favre says. "But we finally did it and, believe me, they're still good."[38]

The Packers clinched their third NFC Central Division title in a row with a 7–6 win over Tampa Bay on December 7. Favre was so loose during the game that he did not even let the taunting of defender Warren Sapp get under his skin. When Sapp rushed him and warned Favre that he would be after him all day, Favre gave Sapp a pat on his rotund stomach and said, "With that tummy, I don't think you're going to make it."[39]

The team finished the season with a 13–3 record and made it to the playoffs for the fifth year in a row. Favre made plays work any way he could, keeping the ball himself if it meant that was the only way he could help the team pick up yardage. The determined quarterback finished the season with 187 yards (171m) and fifty-eight carries and was the team's second-leading rusher.

Playoff Champs

Favre won his third MVP award after the 1997 season, sharing it with Detroit Lions running back Barry Sanders. Once again his leadership skills came through in the playoffs. On January 4 the Packers faced Tampa Bay in the divisional playoff game in Green Bay. For the first score of the game, Favre led the team 67 yards (61m) down the field and hit tight end Mark Chmura for a touchdown. Favre threw two interceptions and was sacked three times by Warren Sapp but still managed to throw for 190 yards (174m) and score the final points of the contest. He made it into the end zone on a quarterback draw to score a two-point conversion after a touchdown by Dorsey Levens. The Packers won 21–7, setting the stage for a matchup against the San Francisco 49ers in the NFC championship game.

The night before the game in San Francisco, Favre was nervous about facing the 49er defense. "I said more prayers before this game than before any game I ever remember," he says. "We were playing a great game with a great defense, and I just prayed that I'd play smart and make good decisions."[40]

Favre's prayers were answered as he drove the team 68 yards (62m) down the field to set up the first score of the game, a 19-yard (17m) field goal by Ryan Longwell. Early in the second quarter, Eugene Robinson intercepted a 49er pass and returned it to the San Francisco 28-yard (26m) line. Favre found Antonio Freeman on the left side of the field, and the receiver sped into the end zone to give the Packers a 10–0 lead. Favre sidestepped 49er blitzes and threw for 222 yards (203m) that day, consistently hitting receivers Brooks and Freeman with crisp passes. The Packers dominated the contest and won 23–10. The team was on its way to its second Super Bowl in two years.

Super Bust

The Packers were double-digit favorites as they faced the Denver Broncos in Super Bowl XXXII at San Diego's Qualcomm Stadium on January 25, 1998. The sentimental vote went to the Broncos' John Elway in the matchup, however. He had lost three previous Super Bowls with the Broncos, and this was likely his final appearance in the big game. Nonetheless, Favre and the Packers were loose and confident that they could beat the Broncos. Favre felt relaxed enough to joke about how eating antelope two nights before the big game might affect the way he played.

At first, it looked like he would have another stellar performance. He hit Freeman with a 22-yard (20m) pass to end the team's opening drive with a touchdown. However, he also tossed an interception in the first quarter, and the Broncos led at halftime 17–14.

In the second half, the Packers managed to tie the score with a field goal after a Denver fumble, but Denver scored a touchdown as the third quarter drew to a close. Although the Packers fumbled the kickoff, Packer Eugene Robinson intercepted Elway's pass in the end zone. With 13.5 minutes to go, Favre drove the team 85 yards (78m) down the field to again tie the score.

It did not take the Broncos long to answer. Elway drove the Broncos to the Packers' 1-yard (.9m) line with one minute and forty-seven seconds left to play. Holmgren let the Broncos score to give his team time for one more drive. Favre could not get it done, though. The Broncos' defense had been studying how Favre played and knew how to cover him. "We saw how many chances he takes," says Denver cornerback Ray Crockett. "He's succeeded on most of those chances the last few years and gained tremendous confidence. By being a risk-taker, he's become the greatest quarterback in the game. But what made him great got him in trouble against us."[41] This time, Favre's risks did not pay off. He threw three incomplete passes, and the Broncos won 31–24.

Two future Hall of Famers, Favre and Denver's John Elway, meet on the field before Super Bowl XXXII. Elway's Broncos would prevail in the contest 31–24.

The loss was a huge disappointment for Favre. After the game, he felt like going home and going to bed. Instead, he went to a restaurant with his wife, daughter, and some other relatives. He reflected on what he had in his life that was more important than football. "Thank God for you and Brittany," his wife says he commented. "At that moment, I knew that my husband had begun to realize that family was more important than football, and that we'd be there for him when he was finished with the game,"[42] Deanna Favre recalls.

Comeback Stalled

As difficult as that defeat was, Favre believed the team would rebound. He was confident the loss would serve to make the team hungry for a Super Bowl win the next season. "This should serve as a wakeup call for this team," he later said. "You hate to get it in the Super Bowl, but we're young. Sometimes, when you're young, you think you're too good. But this is a great football team, and there's no reason we shouldn't be back to more Super Bowls."[43]

In 1998 Favre focused his energy on winning another league championship. He proved that he remained resilient when he was sacked by Regan Upshaw in the team's second game of the season against Tampa Bay on September 13. He came back to throw a 38-yard (35m) touchdown pass to Antonio Freeman two plays after the sack. The Packers won 23–15.

The risks Favre was prone to take both helped and hurt him and the team. He threw an interception on his first pass attempt in the team's September 27 game against Carolina, but despite throwing three interceptions in the game, he also threw for five touchdowns. He threw for a total of 388 yards (355m) in the 37–30 win.

Favre also threw three interceptions the next week against the Vikings, as the Packers faced a strong rival for the division title. With the addition of talented receiver Randy Moss, the Vikings were emerging as a powerful opponent in the NFC Central Division. The Packers got a taste of his talent in the 37–24 loss on October 5. It was the Packers' first loss at home since the first game of the 1995 season.

The Vikings again beat the Packers in the Metrodome on November 22 and won the division title. The Packers finished the regular season 11–5, taking second in their division and securing a spot in the NFC wild card game. Favre was on top of the league's quarterbacks statistically, leading with 4,212 passing yards (3,851m) and 347 completions. However, he also threw twenty-three interceptions, the most he had thrown since 1993.

Favre and his Packers suffered their first loss in a playoff game to the San Francisco 49ers on January 3, 1999.

The Packers faced San Francisco in the first round of the playoffs, taking on the 49ers at 3Com Park on January 3, 1999. The Packers had beat the 49ers five times in a row, and it looked like the team was in a great position for another victory. The Packers got the ball with four minutes and nineteen seconds left to go. The team was behind 23–20, and a 47-yard (43m) pass from Favre to Corey Bradford moved the team to scoring range. A few plays later Favre audibled a route that sent Antonio Freeman sprinting down the field. He hit him with a 15-yard (14m) touchdown pass to cap an 89-yard (81m) drive with a touchdown with one minute and fifty-six seconds left in the game.

The Packers led 27–23, but the 49ers responded with a drive of their own. Steve Young directed the team down the field in the final two minutes of the game. He engineered a 76-yard (69m) drive that ended with a 25-yard (23m) touchdown pass to Terrell Owens. The play put the 49ers up 30–27 with three seconds left, and the Packers' postseason was cut short. It was the first time in six years the Packers had not won a playoff game.

Changes in Green Bay

The loss was heartbreaking for Packers fans, who had gotten used to seeing Favre drive their team deep into the playoffs. The failure to advance in the playoffs for the first time in six years was only the first of a number of changes the team would have to endure. Three days after the loss to San Francisco, Coach Holmgren announced he was leaving the Packers. He headed to Seattle to be both coach and general manager of the Seahawks. He had been Favre's mentor, channeling his enthusiasm and tendency to try to force plays into a productive style that helped him become one of the league's great quarterbacks. Now Favre would be without his guidance. Favre had expected Holmgren's exit and was ready to make the best of the situation. "Early on he stuck with me longer than any other coach would have," Favre says. "But we've got to keep going."[44]

Holmgren was not the only person to leave the team, however. Quarterbacks coach Andy Reid went to the Philadelphia Eagles, and strength coach Kent Johnson went to Seattle with Holmgren. The team lost a leader on defense as well, as Pro Bowl defensive end Reggie White also left the Packers after the 1998 season.

Making Changes

While many of the people who had guided Favre's career were moving on, he took steps to try to prevent his career from slipping. He had always enjoyed going out with his friends and drinking, and while he had stopped for several months after his stint in rehab, he had started partying with his friends once again. Now, however, he realized that he needed to change. He admitted that he had an alcohol problem and stopped drinking. As he neared thirty, he realized how alcohol was having a negative impact on his family life, and he realized that drinking would make it more difficult for him to compete with the younger players he was facing. "I'll be 30 this year and I don't want to be the forgotten man,"[45] he said at the time.

Favre helps his wife with cooking at their home. Favre's life away from football increasingly revolved around his family as he neared the age of thirty.

Favre also had another reason to give up drinking. Drinking and partying weighed on his family life, and his wife, Deanna, was pregnant with their second child. She had undergone infertility treatments, and Favre had supported Deanna as the couple had gone through the emotional highs and lows of dealing with infertility. She gave birth to their second daughter, Breleigh Ann, in July. "I've lived a fun, hard life," Favre said. "But fun now is watching [my ten-year-old daughter, Brittany] play softball. Fun is having rookies in the weight room look at me as an example of what they want to be. I'm done with alcohol."[46]

Out of Steam

Although he prepared as best he could, the 1999 season was a painful one for Favre and the Packers. Ray Rhodes, the team's defensive coordinator, took over as head coach, and offensive coordinator Sherm Lewis called the plays. The team struggled, and Favre played much of the season with a nagging injury. He sprained the right thumb on his throwing hand on August 23 in a preseason game against Denver. He hurt it again on September 12 against Oakland, the Packers' opening-day game. He displayed his typical grit and determination by staying in the game, despite hitting his sore thumb on the helmet of Russell Maryland of Oakland early in the second half. With one minute and forty-nine seconds left in the game, he drove the Packers 82 yards (75m) down the field for the winning score, a 1-yard (.9m) touchdown pass to tight end Jeff Thomason with eleven seconds on the clock. The Packers won 28–24.

Favre also got revenge for the pair of losses Minnesota handed the Packers the previous season. In the final minutes of the September 26 game against the Vikings, the Packers needed to go 77 yards (70m) to reach the end zone. Favre took the Packers down the field. At fourth down and 1 yard (.9m) to go, with no timeouts, he threw a 23-yard (21m) touchdown pass to Bradford with twelve seconds left. The Packers won 23–20.

Favre celebrated his thirtieth birthday on national television, in a game against Tampa Bay. With less than two minutes to play, the Packers trailed the Buccaneers. Favre threw a 42-yard (38m) bullet up the left sideline to wide receiver Bill Schroeder to start a 73-yard (67m) drive. He drove the team down the field forty seconds, lofting a 21-yard (19m) touchdown pass to Antonio Freeman while under pressure from a Tampa Bay blitz. The Packers' final score came with one minute and five seconds left in the game, and the team won 26–23.

Favre also had frustrating moments that season, however. He had one of his worst games against the Denver Broncos on October 17, completing only seven of twenty-three passes for 120 yards (110m). He threw three interceptions as the Packers lost the game 31–10. Favre reached the 30,000-yard (27,432m) passing mark against Carolina on December 12. Although he threw for 300 yards (274m) that day and carried the ball five times to pick up first downs, the team lost 31–33. It was another in a series of disappointing games

A Kind Heart

Brett followed his parents' advice both on and off the field. Irv Favre taught him about toughness, and Bonita Favre taught him to be concerned for others. Bonita taught special education and stressed to her children that the developmentally disabled students she taught deserved respect. Brett took her words to heart.

A developmentally disabled man would help Irv Favre as equipment manager, and while he was still in high school Brett included him in conversations and did not feel uncomfortable sharing a table with him at a restaurant. He knew the other students looked up to him as the football team's quarterback, and he wanted to impress upon them the attitude of equality his mother had instilled in him. Brett and the man, Ronnie Hebert, formed a lasting friendship. After Favre became a pro football player, his wife surprised Favre by inviting Hebert to speak at a fund-raising dinner. His friend's surprise appearance touched the quarterback's heart, Deanna Favre says.

for Favre and the team that season. The Packers finished fourth in the five-team NFC Central Division. Favre threw for more interceptions than touchdowns that season (twenty-three interceptions and twenty-two touchdowns) as the team went 8–8. For the first time in seven years, the Packers did not make the playoffs.

The road to his second Super Bowl had seemed effortless, but Favre had learned that staying on top is much more difficult than getting there. As the team struggled to reclaim the dominance it had enjoyed, Favre worked hard to prolong his career. He still loved playing the game, and he played with pain as he continued to give the NFL its share of exciting moments.

Chapter Five

Triumph and Tragedy

The Packers turned in a new direction in 2000, hiring Coach Mike Sherman to lead the team. Sherman tried to restore the Packers to the Super Bowl contenders they had been only a few seasons earlier, and some wondered whether Favre was up to the challenge. He had started in 125 games in a row as quarterback, more than any other quarterback in NFL history, but had developed tendinitis in his throwing arm. Favre had no doubt that he would be able to keep going however. "I know people are saying my best days are behind me," he said at the time. "But I've got a lot more to accomplish in this game. I'll play again, and I'll play well."[47]

Sherman began turning the Packers into a Super Bowl team and worked to regain the success it took to make it back to the playoffs. As the team came tantalizingly close to a return to the Super Bowl, Favre's personal life took a tragic turn. He dealt with losses and family crises that were much more difficult than anything he dealt with on the field. Playing football became a welcome escape as he dealt with tragedy in his personal life.

Rebuilding

In 2000 Favre's mind was on his new coach and his elbow. He adjusted to Sherman's coaching style, but injuries continued to test the quarterback's mettle. He sat out three preseason games to rest his arm because of his tendinitis. After resting for two weeks,

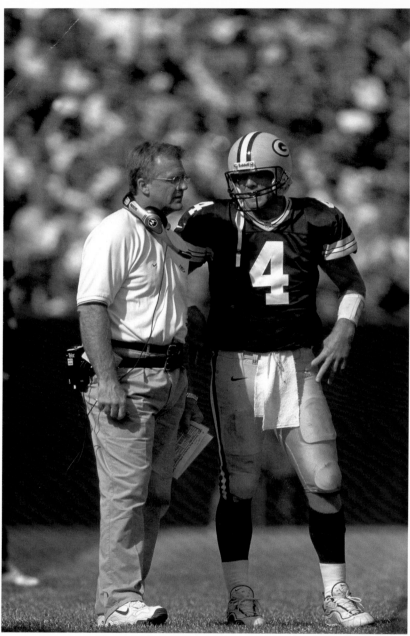

In 2000 the Packers hired Mike Sherman, left, as head coach. Although Favre adjusted to Sherman's coaching style, he was plagued by nagging injuries that affected his play.

he started throwing again on August 23 and was ready for the season opener.

The Packers lost the first two games of the season to the New York Jets and Buffalo Bills respectively, but Favre showed that he still could bring the team from behind to victory against the Philadelphia Eagles on September 17. In the final five minutes of the game, Favre led the Packers on a 60-yard (55m) drive to give the Packers a 6–3 win. He was sacked five times that day but still managed to pass for 189 yards (173m).

The Packers' season record stood at 3–5 when Favre put his acrobatic passing ability on display against the Vikings on November 6. The gutsy quarterback passed for two touchdowns that day. One was an underhanded 5-yard (4.6m) toss to Ahman Green and the other was a 43-yard (39m) pass that sailed into the hands of Antonio Freeman in overtime to give the Packers the win.

Favre seemed to do his best when people counted him out. Another injury, resulting from a sack by the Buccaneers' Warren Sapp, on November 12 took him out of the game in the third quarter with a foot sprain. He returned the next week against Indianapolis, however, and threw for 301 yards (275m) as the Packers beat the Indianapolis Colts 26–24.

The Buccaneers and Vikings were the teams to beat in the NFC Central Division that year, and in the closing weeks of the season, the Packers managed to best both teams. Favre threw for 290 yards (265m) and three touchdowns against the Vikings, leading the Packers to a 33–28 win in the Minneapolis Metrodome on December 17. The following week, the Packers beat the Buccaneers 17–14. The Packers finished with a 9–7 record, third in the NFC Central, but the team did not make the playoffs for the second year in a row. Injuries could not stop Favre, but the team as a whole was not quite good enough to compete with the best.

Packer Forever

Despite the team's disappointing third-place finish in the Central Division, the Packers still valued Favre and his contributions to the team. The thirty-one-year-old quarterback signed a lifetime contract with the Packers on March 1, 2001. He said he could not envision himself playing with any other team, and his coach agreed. "No player in the NFL identifies, or is more closely linked to, a specific team like Brett Favre is to the Green Bay Packers," Sherman said. "He embodies the spirit and character to Packer fans everywhere. I do not think there is a player in the NFL that experiences a relationship with the fans like Brett Favre does."[48]

Fans had more to cheer about in 2001, as the Packers improved their record and returned to the playoffs. With the win over the Baltimore Ravens on October 14, Favre showed that he could still hold his own against the best defenders in the league. The Ravens had won the Super Bowl the previous year, and in the first four games of the season they had allowed only three touchdown drives, which all resulted from accidental turnovers. Favre dominated the Ravens' defense, throwing for 337 yards (308m) and three touchdowns. "When you see him in person it's kind of like Michael Jordan," says Ravens tight end Shannon Sharpe. "When Brett drops back, you just expect him to complete a pass. And he's as good as I've seen at the position in my 12 years in the league."[49]

A few weeks later, Favre displayed the offensive pizzazz that made him such an exciting player. On November 11 the team faced the first-place Chicago Bears, and Favre threw for 268 yards (245m). His passes included a 41-yard (37m) bomb to Bill Schroeder at the back left corner of the end zone as the first half wound down. The Packers won 20–12.

The Packers regained momentum in 2001, going 12–4 in the regular season and returning to postseason play for the first time since the 1998 wild card playoff game. According to Sherman, Favre's play improved that season, as he made better decisions on the field. "He's done a great job of being judgmental with the football and taking the shots we need to take," Sherman says. "He's being aggressive, which he always is, but he's being careful at the same time."[50]

Favre showed that aggression the next week during the Packers' NFC wild card playoff game against the San Francisco 49ers. The Packers trailed 7–6 at halftime, but Favre led the team to four second-half scoring drives. The Packers won 25–15. At halftime,

In the 2001 NFC divisional playoff game, Favre threw a career high six interceptions in the Packers' 45–17 drubbing by the St. Louis Rams.

Favre had some inspirational words for his teammates. As Favre later recalled, "I don't ever want to look back and say we left something on the field. . . . I said 'Let's go get them. Let's lay it on the field. When we come off the field, don't ever look back and say we should have taken some chances or should have done this or that.' And I think we played that way."[51]

Favre's risky and exciting style turned reckless the following week against the St. Louis Rams, however. In the 2001 NFC divisional playoff game on January 20, he threw six interceptions, matching an NFL record. Three of the interceptions were returned for touchdowns, and the Packers lost 45–17.

Player of the Year

Favre managed to put the tough playoff loss behind him and get ready for the next season. In the first game of the year, against the Atlanta Falcons, he showed that he maintained the confidence that made him a great quarterback. He threw for two touchdowns and led the Packers to a 37–34 overtime win.

He again proved that he could make the big play in a Monday night game at Chicago on October 7. He found wide receiver Donald Driver and hit him with an 85-yard (78m) pass for his first of three touchdowns in the game. He threw for 359 yards (328m), as the Packers won 32–21.

The next week against the New England Patriots, Favre became the fourth player in NFL history to throw three hundred career touchdown passes. When he sprained a ligament in his knee on October 20, however, it looked like the Packers' season and Favre's streak as the starting quarterback would be in jeopardy. The team had the following week off, giving Favre a little more time to heal, and he was the team's starter when it faced the Miami Dolphins on November 4. On Monday Night Football, Favre led the team to a 24–10 win, throwing for 187 yards (171m) and a touchdown.

The Packers finished the season 12–4. Favre was *Sports Illustrated*'s NFL Player of the Year and the leading candidate in the balloting for the upcoming Pro Bowl, football's all-star game. The team was on top of its new division, the NFC North, and was

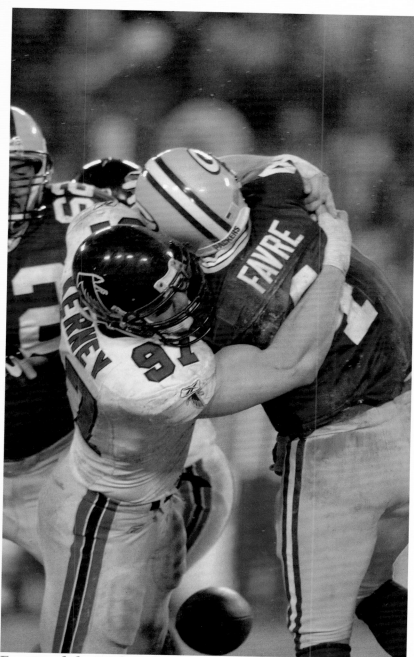

Favre and the Packers lost their first playoff game at Lambeau Field to the Atlanta Falcons in January 2002.

optimistic heading into the playoffs. The team was 8–0 at home and had never lost a playoff game at Lambeau Field.

On a snowy January day in Green Bay, however, it was Michael Vick rather than Favre who led his team to victory. Vick and the Atlanta Falcons led the Packers 24–0 by halftime. Favre found Donald Driver with a 14-yard (12.8m) touchdown pass on the team's first drive of the second half, but Favre also had two interceptions and a fumble in the game. The touchdown to Driver was the only score the Packers could manage, and the team lost to the Falcons 27–7.

Heartache and Glory

The Packers continued to press toward the playoffs the next season, but a personal tragedy overshadowed anything that happened to Favre on the football field. The first three quarters of the season were up and down for Favre. He threw glorious touchdown passes, such as a sideline pass to wide receiver Javon Walker for a 66-yard (60m) score against the 49ers on November 23. But he also tossed interception after interception, including three against Detroit on Thanksgiving.

A thumb injury again brought grief. Favre fractured his right thumb on October 19 during a game at St. Louis, when he hit the shoulder pad of Packers guard Mike Wahle. He stayed in the game and threw for two touchdowns, but after the game doctors recommended that he have surgery to place pins in his thumb. This would ensure that it healed properly, but he would be out for four to six weeks. Instead of having the surgery, Favre nursed the broken thumb during an off-week and returned for a Sunday night game against Minnesota on November 2. He threw for three touchdowns, and Green Bay won 30–27.

Any success he had on the field that season was dimmed by a tragedy in Favre's personal life. The Packers made a trip to Oakland to play the Raiders that December. The day before the Monday night game, Favre and some teammates went out for a round of golf. He was on the golf course on December 21, 2003, when his wife called to tell him his father had died. Irv Favre had suffered a heart attack while driving to his home in Kiln. Favre was shocked at the loss of the man who had coached him and remained close to him during his professional career. "I couldn't imagine never seeing my dad again, just like I couldn't imagine him never watching me play football again,"[52] Favre says.

Teammate Ahman Green embraces an emotional Favre after passing for 311 yards and 4 touchdowns in a win over Oakland in a game played the day after his father Irv passed away.

Coach Sherman told Favre that he would support his decision if Favre decided to go home to be with this family at this difficult time. However, Favre knew that the Packers needed to win that game if they were to stay in the race for the playoffs. He knew his teammates were counting on him and that his father had valued commitment to the team. After his wife and mother encouraged him to play, Favre agreed to stay in Oakland.

Favre had no idea how the loss of his father would impact his play on the field. He was nervous about how he would perform, and thoughts of the loss of his father continually crept in. Rather than collapsing under the weight of his grief, Favre channeled his emotions into an amazing performance. In the first half, he threw

Retirement?

In early 2002 a postseason loss and the demands of preseason workouts began to wear on Favre. He still loved playing the game, but as he prepared for his twelfth NFL season, thoughts of leaving the NFL crept in. Rumors of a possible retirement began to surface. "I think about retirement a heck of a lot more than I used to," he said at the time.

Favre was still excited about playing games and about the season to come, but he would rather be home on his property in Hattiesburg, Mississippi, than in training camp. Favre's competitive nature had many wondering if he would actually follow through on his thoughts after the season, however. In addition, if he stayed in the league he had the chance to break numerous records. He indicated that it was not records that compelled him to keep playing, however. "If I thought like that, I'd be playing for the wrong reason," he says. "I don't play football to pass Dan Marino. I play to compete and win. That's why I've been successful. If I were basking in what I've done, there would be a lot to bask in. But I don't care. When the season's over, it's over."

Quoted in *Sports Illustrated,* "Quittin' Time?" September 9, 2002, p. 70.

for 311 yards (284m) and four touchdowns. He made spectacular throws, and his receivers responded with incredible plays. After finding tight end Wesley Walls in the corner of the end zone for the first touchdown of the night, he embraced his teammate. "I knew that once the game was over I still had to deal with Dad's death, with my emotions, with my family, and I couldn't expect other people to still feel what I was feeling," he says. "That's probably why I was so happy for Wesley. I didn't want to take anything away from what the other guys were doing."[53]

Favre ended the game with 399 yards (365m) and no interceptions. The Packers won 41–7. "I knew that my dad would have wanted me to play. I love him so much and I love this game. It's meant a great deal to me, to my dad, to my family, and I didn't expect this kind of performance,"[54] Favre says.

The Packers ended the season with a 10–6 record and a division title. Favre continued to play well into the playoffs. He set a new NFL record for consecutive postseason games with a touchdown pass on January 4, 2004, in a wild card playoff game against the Seattle Seahawks. Although the Packers lost the divisional playoff game the next week to the Philadelphia Eagles, with a score of 20–17, Favre had proven that he remained a powerful force in the NFL.

Strength in Difficult Times

It looked like the momentum the Packers had at the end of the 2003 season would carry into 2004. "I still love playing," Favre said at the time. "And there's no doubt in my mind I can lead this team to the Super Bowl, and win it."[55] It looked like he was right when the team beat the defending NFC champion Carolina Panthers 24–14 on Monday Night Football. However, the team lost four games in a row after that.

As he dealt with the team's disappointing start to the season, Favre faced more heartbreaking times off the field. His wife's brother, Casey, was killed in an all-terrain vehicle crash in Mississippi. A few days later, his wife learned she had breast cancer.

As difficult as this news was to hear, Favre and his family forged ahead. He reassured his wife as she had surgery to remove the

In July of 2004 Favre's wife Deanna accepted an ESPY award for best moment for her fight against breast cancer.

cancerous tumor, and afterward he helped her count down the days until her chemotherapy treatments were done.

On the field, Favre and the Packers turned things around. The state of Wisconsin celebrated its popular quarterback on November 29, which was proclaimed Brett Favre Day. Favre started his two-hundredth consecutive NFL game that day, and the Packers beat the St. Louis Rams on Monday Night Football. Favre threw for three touchdowns in the 45–17 win.

The Packers claimed their third straight division title with a win over the Minnesota Vikings on Christmas Eve. Favre's performance that day was both frustrating and incredible. The Vikings went ahead 31–24 with eight minutes and eighteen seconds left on the clock after Favre threw an interception that was returned 15 yards (13.7m) for a touchdown. However, he came back with an 80-yard (73m) drive that ended with a 3-yard (2.7m) touchdown pass to Donald Driver on fourth down. Then, with less than two minutes remaining, he again took the Packers down the field. The Viking blitz was closing in when he found Javon Walker on the sideline. He got the pass off just before he was hit. Walker went 31 yards (28m) up the sideline, and Ryan Longwell capped the 76-yard (69m) drive with a field goal to give the Packers the win.

Favre ended the day with three touchdowns, and the Packers had their third straight NFC North division title. "Never give up," Favre said. "That's been this team's M.O. [operating mode] all season, because we could have quit a long time ago."[56]

A Fighter

The Packers finished the season with a 10–6 record. Favre threw for 4,000 yards (3,658m), for the fourth time as a pro and the first time since 1999. The postseason brought more disappointment, as the Packers faced the Vikings in the wild card playoff game. Favre threw four interceptions, and the team lost, 31–17.

After the season ended, Favre continued to support his wife as she finished her chemotherapy treatments in January and went through radiation therapy in February. The treatments made her tired, but they were successful in ridding her body of cancer.

The Game on His Mind

One of the most unusual examples of Favre's dedication to staying in the game came on October 3, 2004, in a matchup against the New York Giants. After being hit hard on the first drive of the second half, he left the game but ran back onto the field two plays later, without clearance from team doctors. On fourth down and 5 yards (4.6m) to go, he threw a 28-yard (26m) touchdown pass to wide receiver Javon Walker. After the Packers scored, doctors kept Favre out of the game because of a concussion. Despite Favre's determination, the team lost 14–7.

Favre suffered another personal blow just before the start of the next season. In August 2005 Hurricane Katrina flooded his childhood home in Kiln. His family survived, but the trophies and awards he had won as a child were destroyed, as was his childhood home. It was yet another emotional challenge for the athlete. As he battled through painful personal times, he earned the respect of players, coaches, and fans.

Chapter Six

Record Player

Favre had endured difficult times both on and off the field but, while he had considered retirement, he was not yet ready to give up the game of football in 2005. He was still physically able to play and loved heading out to the field on Sunday. He enjoyed relaxing at home in the off-season, but as football season neared, the desire to get back onto the field pulled him into the game.

Questions about when he would retire hung in the air, but Favre had things to accomplish before he answered them. He repeatedly said he did not play to get his name in the record book, but at the same time, he wanted to make sure he made his mark on the game he loved. His toughness and longevity had elevated him to legendary status, and he was on his way to eclipsing every significant quarterback record.

Favre's mind was on things other than football right before the 2005 season started, however. After Hurricane Katrina hit the Gulf Coast in August 2005, Favre made sure his family was safe and then used the Packers' press conferences to ask for help for his home state. Donations of money and supplies came in, and Packers fans even headed to Mississippi to deliver food, water, and clothing. Favre also arranged for donations to be flown and trucked to Mississippi. He felt a responsibility to do what he could to help.

Down but Not Out

Favre also tried hard to do what he could for the Packers in 2005, but his efforts to bring the team a victory often came up short.

Relief workers distribute aid to Hurricane Katrina victims that was donated by Favre and his supporters.

While Favre continued to enjoy playing football, the troubles of the previous year and injuries to his teammates led to a poor season for the quarterback and the Packers in 2005. Favre was in great physical shape, throwing a league-leading 362 passes that year. He also rushed for 62 yards (57m) during the season, more than he had rushed for in the previous two years combined. However, too many games went the way of a loss at Carolina on October 3. Favre threw for 303 yards (277m) and four touchdowns and was poised to score on the Packers' final drive with a minute

Identifying with a Hero

Throughout the ups and downs of his career, Favre remained a popular figure in Green Bay. He was a hero the fans could understand. "People here treat us like family, and I think they care for us like family," Deanna Favre once said. "Because of everything we've been through, they don't see Brett as untouchable or some kind of superhero. And they've been through it with us. The fans here feel close to Brett because they've had their own similar struggles."

Alan Shipnuck, "Sportsman of the Year," *Sports Illustrated,* December 10, 2007, p. 42.

Throughout his Packer career, Favre always enjoyed unwavering support from Packer fans.

left. It looked like the perfect situation for Favre, and fans had come to expect big last-second plays from the veteran. However, on fourth down and 2 yards (1.8m) to go, his pass to Donald Driver was incomplete.

A personal low for Favre came on October 30 in a game against Cincinnati, in which he threw a career-high five interceptions. He also had a four-interception game on Christmas Day against Chicago, including one to end the game. Favre threw a league-leading twenty-nine interceptions that year, a statistic that some said showed more about his desire to win than his fading ability as a quarterback. When the team fell behind, he became a reckless gunslinger, taking risks as he tried to make plays that he thought could get his team back into the game. "In games when they're behind, a lot of quarterbacks pack it in and protect their stats," says Ted Thompson, the Packers' general manager. "Brett was still trying even when the odds were tall."[57]

Favre's risky plays did not help the Packers' record that season. The team ended the season at 4–12, last in the NFC North. Sportswriter Tom Silverstein gave the Packers' offense an "F" for the season and summed up their play this way: "Favre played like a rookie at times, the line underachieved, and receivers were injured."[58]

A New Direction

The dismal season led to the departure of Coach Mike Sherman. Mike McCarthy, who had been the Packers' quarterbacks coach in 1999, took over as the team's head coach in 2006. There was speculation that Favre would step aside and let the team rebuild without him under a new coach. Favre himself was unsure about what he would do. "There's days I wake up and say, 'You know what? I can't retire. Don't be stupid. What will I do?'" he said in January during an ESPN interview. "There's other days I go, 'What if it's crunch time, 2 minutes left, do you want the ball?' I don't know if I do."[59]

Favre knew he was still capable of playing and competing, and he could not resist returning to the game. In April that year he announced his decision to stay with the team. Before the season, he admitted that his body felt the effects of fifteen years in the league, but he said his arm felt great. "I know I can still play," he said, and he indicated that he was optimistic about the coming season despite playing on a team with many young, unproven players. "If we can somehow put it together, there's a lot of talent out there."[60]

The Packers' inexperience was on display in the season opener when they lost to the Chicago Bears 26–0. It was Favre's first shutout as a pro quarterback. However, a slow start to the season did not dull Favre's love to compete. The team took a 1–4 record to Miami on October 22, and things looked rough for the team when Favre had the football knocked from his hand at the beginning of the contest. The Packers were behind 10–6 at halftime, but a third-quarter interception by Green Bay cornerback Charles Woodson put the team ahead. Later that quarter, Favre threw a pass between two defenders to hit receiver Donald Driver. The play was initially called incomplete, but the Packers challenged. When it was overturned, Favre was so excited that he twirled Driver on his shoulders. The Packers went on to win, 34–24, and Favre sealed the victory with a pass to tight end David Martin for a 13-yard (11.8m) touchdown.

That year Favre became the first NFL quarterback to throw five thousand completions. The record came on his last pass of the night in a 9–7 win over Minnesota on December 21. The win was part of the team's four-game winning streak at the end of the season, which was good enough to earn it second place in the NFC North division with an 8–8 record. The team did not make the playoffs, however, and while Favre cut his interception total to eighteen and played better than he had the previous season, he still had his moments of failure. "He was excellent at times, awful at others," sportswriter Mike Woods says. "At best, he was consistently inconsistent."[61]

When interviewed after the final game of the season on December 31, Favre had tears in his eyes as he spoke. He was again thinking about retiring. He posed for a photo with his offensive linemen after the game but would not say if it was his last NFL contest. Favre had finished the season just shy of breaking some of the biggest records in NFL history, and he was the leader of a young team that appeared to be on the cusp of significant achievements. Now he

Packer receiver Greg Jennings carries the ball from Favre's all-time NFL record-breaking 421st touchdown pass into the end zone on September 30, 2007.

had to look within himself to see if he still had the heart and determination to lead the team for another year.

A Star Is Reborn

In early February 2007 Favre let the team and fans know that he would be back for another season. Teammate Nick Barnett was not surprised. "We were on such a huge run and he had to believe we were on the verge of doing something big,"[62] Barnett says.

After two subpar seasons, fans and commentators did not expect a great deal from the Packers at the beginning of the 2007 season. Coach McCarthy challenged Favre to put more effort into preparing for games. Favre accepted the challenge and worked out for four months at his Mississippi home with a personal trainer. After the season started, he fell into a regimented routine. He diligently studied film of his opponents, and soon after one game was finished, he began preparing for the next one.

Favre's dedicated efforts led to one of the best seasons of his career. He made history week after week, as NFL records fell under the weight of his strong arm. In the second week of the season, Favre took the title of the NFL's winningest quarterback, passing John Elway's record with a 35–13 victory over the New York Giants.

Two weeks later another record fell. Favre found wide receiver Greg Jennings during the first quarter of the September 30 contest against the Minnesota Vikings. The noise level in the Metrodome was deafening as Favre rifled a 16-yard (14.6m) pass to him for his 421st career touchdown pass, surpassing former Dolphins quarterback Dan Marino as the NFL's all-time touchdown pass leader. When Favre realized he had the record, he was so excited that he ran to the end zone, picked up Jennings, and carried him on his shoulders. He hugged his teammates and went to the sidelines to hug his wife, Deanna. "It was great, but I've never considered myself as good a quarterback as Dan Marino," Favre said after the game, which the Packers won 23–16. "To be mentioned in the same breath as Dan and other guys really makes it special."[63]

Favre also broke Marino's career passing-attempts record, tossing his 8,359th pass in the second quarter against Minnesota. The graying Favre did not look like the same quarterback who had appeared to be trailing off at the end of his career only a couple seasons earlier. His passion for football inspired his younger teammates. "Any time you have a guy who's out there who has played 17 years and is 37 years old running around and having fun, he makes us go," Jennings says. "Just to see him with that type of enthusiasm and excitement, he puts the buzz in everybody else."[64]

Several more records were within Favre's grasp, but rather than concentrating on personal statistics, Coach McCarthy said he saw that Favre had a different goal in mind that season. "The big thing with him is January football," McCarthy said about the time in the season when playoff games arrive. "You look in his eyes, and you can see the wars he's been through, trying to get to more January football. It's all he cares about."[65]

Whether he was aiming for them or not, more records fell as the season progressed. On November 22, Favre threw three touchdowns in a win over the Lions, setting a new record for the most NFL games with three or more touchdown passes with sixty-three games. Against the Rams on December 16, he surpassed Marino's record for career passing yards, with 61,367 (56,114m). By the end of the season, he had thrown for a total of 61,655 yards (56,377m) in his career. He also had achieved 160 wins and 442 touchdowns. He had his best passer rating since 1996, and he led the team to a 13–3 record and first place in the NFC North for the team's eighteenth division title. As he had hoped, the Packers would be playing in January.

What to Do with Favre's Locker?

For months in 2008, after he had said he was retiring, Favre's nameplate remained above his locker at Lambeau Field. The field had been refurbished in 2002, and Favre had been the only player to ever use the locker. The team decided that he should be the only player to ever use the locker and gave it to him.

The team planned to remove the locker and send it to Favre so he could display it at his home in Mississippi. "We thought anybody who played 16 years here as well as he did might want his own locker," says Packers general manager Ted Thompson. "I think it makes it a little easier, quite frankly, for the next guy to go into there." He adds, "I mean, you can't really put anybody in his locker."

Associated Press, "Packers to Deliver Old Locker to Favre," *USA Today*, May 29, 2008. www.usatoday.com.

Let It Snow

Snowflakes swirled through the air as the Packers faced the Seattle Seahawks in the NFC divisional playoff game at Lambeau Field on January 13, 2008. The snowfall got heavier as the game went on, covering the field with a blanket of white. "I've been hoping for that for 17 years," Favre said. "I watched the weather all day. I'm like, 'Just give us one of those big snow games.'"[66]

The Packers initially looked like they would be snowed under, as running back Ryan Grant fumbled twice early in the game and the Packers were down 14–0 before five minutes of the game had expired. Favre consoled Grant on the sidelines, telling his teammate, "Hey, you know what? Believe me if there's one person who knows what it feels like to be in your shoes, it's me." Favre advised him to "go down swinging,"[67] and Grant did, subsequently rushing for 201 yards (184m) and three touchdowns. His first came at the end of the first quarter, on a 1-yard (.9m) touchdown run after Favre drove the team 64 yards (59m) in nine plays. Near the end of the half, Favre stumbled as he flipped an underhanded pass to Donald Lee for an 11-yard (10m) gain. Grant scored a touchdown on the next play, and the Packers took a 28–17 lead at halftime.

Favre threw for another touchdown in the second half, and Grant ran for one to give the Packers a 42–20 victory. The game was simply a lot of fun for Favre, as the thirty-eight-year-old playfully threw snowballs at Donald Driver on the sidelines. On a beautiful, snowy afternoon at Lambeau Field, he had taken the Packers to within one game of the Super Bowl.

The End of an Era

The Packers again had home field advantage the next week against the New York Giants as they played for a trip to the Super Bowl. It was a brutally cold game, with a temperature of -3 degrees Fahrenheit (-19C) and a frigid wind that made it feel as cold as -24 degrees Fahrenheit (-31C). It was the third-coldest championship game in NFL history.

The team struggled in the cold weather, but early in the second quarter it appeared that Favre's arm would carry the Packers to victory. The Giants led on a pair of field goals, but on the next series Favre found Driver, who eluded three Giants as he raced 71 yards (65m) to the end zone. Later that quarter, Driver caught a 20-yard (18m) pass from Favre that set up a field goal to put the Packers ahead 10–6 at halftime.

The Giants did not take long to respond, beginning the second half with a 69-yard (63m) scoring drive. A long kickoff return and a penalty on the Giants put Favre and the Packers in position for Favre's second touchdown pass of the day, a 12-yard (10.9m) throw to Lee to give the Packers a 17–13 advantage.

Giants quarterback Eli Manning hit receivers Plaxico Burress and Amani Toomer to move the Giants down the field for another score, and early in the fourth quarter Favre missed an opportunity to put the Packers ahead by throwing an interception as he tried to elude pressure from the Giants' defense. The interception by R.W. McQuarters came back to the Packers after the ball was stripped by Grant and was nabbed by Mark Tauscher, but Favre could not turn the break into a touchdown. The Packers tied the game at 20–20, and after two missed field goals by the Giants, the game went into overtime. "This game, even when it was going back and forth, you just had a sense it was going to fall in place for us again,"[68] Favre says.

That was not to be the case, however. The Packers won the coin toss and took possession, but on the second play of overtime Favre underthrew Driver and was intercepted by Corey Webster. The Giants' Lawrence Tynes hit a field goal, and the Packers' season, and Favre's career in Green Bay came to an end.

His Toughest Call

After the game, Favre said he had not made up his mind about whether he would return for another season. He would have to consult with his family and not let the emotions of the disappointing loss immediately sway him. "I'll try to enjoy this season we had as much as I can, and try to block this game out, which will be very hard,"[69] he said.

Favre had just completed one of the best seasons of his professional career. He set records, made smart decisions on the field, and truly enjoyed playing the game. He was also named *Sports Illustrated*'s

Favre played his last game for the Packers in the NFC Championship game in January 2008.

Sportsman of the Year both for his spectacular playing on the field and his charitable work off it. Favre continued to help children through his charitable foundation, and he regularly set aside time to greet children who asked to meet him through the Make-A-Wish Foundation. He continued to be a leader both on and off the field.

Favre worked as hard as he could at football that season. He had intensely prepared for every contest. However, reaching that level of play was very difficult and draining for the veteran. "I've seen a difference this year," Deanna said. "Mentally and emotionally he is so much more drained. The pressure to keep playing at this high a level gets to him. On Sundays he just goes out and plays, and people only see the love he has for football. During the week I see the strain. He carries the world on his shoulders."[70]

An emotional Favre announces his retirement from football in March 2008. Favre would later change his mind, however, and the Packers traded him to the New York Jets before the start of the 2008 season.

The End Zone

Although the season had been a tiring one for Favre, few expected him to leave the game after the 2007 season. The Packers were close to returning to the Super Bowl and were a young team with a great deal of potential. Favre was in great physical shape and was playing some of the best football of his career. With the Packers so close to the Super Bowl, retirement seemed to be a distant thought for Favre.

However, on March 4, 2008, Favre announced that he would not return to the game. Mentally fatigued, the graying gunslinger decided to retire. He explained that if he returned for another season, the only measure of success would be to win a Super Bowl. He knew it would not be easy for him to achieve that goal, and he did not know if he was up to the challenge. "I know I can still play, but it's like I told my wife, I'm just tired mentally," he said. "I'm just tired."[71]

In a tearful press conference two days later, Favre explained that the only way he could play was to give it everything he had, and he did not know if he still could offer that effort to the Packers. He was fine physically, but he could no longer commit himself to the hours of preparation each game required for him to play to his full potential. He acknowledged that he had a great career and thanked those who had supported him. "It's been everything I thought it would be, and then some. And it's hard to leave," he said. "I've given everything I possibly can give to this organization and I don't think I've got anything left to give, and that's it. I know I can play, but I don't think I want to. And that's really what it comes down to."[72]

A Whole New Ballgame

Favre admitted that he would greatly miss playing the game he loved. For 253 games in a row, over sixteen seasons, he had been the Packers' starting quarterback. Football had been part of his life since he was a child, and now for the first time in decades, he would go into the fall without the need to prepare for a game.

Favre said he had no specific plans for the future, outside of spending more time with his wife and daughters. Hunting, fishing, and spending time on his property in Hattiesburg, Mississippi, were all things he loved to do. During spring and early summer, Favre thought hard about his decision to retire. Soon after he retired there were rumors that he might one day return to the sport he loved, but Favre was noncommittal. "I look forward to whatever the future may hold for me,"[73] he says. It eventually became clear to him that the decision he had made to retire had not been the right one. He talked to the Packers, saying that he wanted to return to football.

The Packers, however, had moved on. After Favre retired, they committed to starting quarterback Aaron Rodgers. Favre would return to football, but not with the team he had been associated with for sixteen years.

Going Out on Top

When Favre left the Packers in 2008, he had a Super Bowl ring, three MVP awards, and numerous records. His accomplishments over seventeen seasons in the NFL included the following:

Ranking first among NFL quarterbacks in regular season wins, with 160.

Being the top-ranked quarterback in career touchdown passes, with 422.

Throwing for the most career passing yards of any NFL quarterback, with 61,655 (56,377m).

Having sixteen seasons with at least 3,000 yards (2,743m) passing.

Ranking first among NFL quarterbacks in career pass completions, with 5,377.

Being the top-ranked NFL quarterback in passing attempts, with 8,758.

Throwing a touchdown pass in eighteen consecutive postseason games.

Having the most career interceptions thrown, with 288.

On August 7, 2008, the Packers traded Favre to the New York Jets. Once he took the field with his new team, he immediately felt at home. He was doing what he loved best and was happy to be on the field where he belonged. "It's like starting all over again,"[74] the veteran quarterback said.

Favre's career was not winding down the way anyone had thought it would. But no matter how long he continued to play the game or where he played it, he would always be known for his durability, his records, and his longevity as a quarterback. And most of all, he would be thought of as a player who had fun playing football and brought excitement to the game every time he stepped on the field.

Notes

Chapter 1: A Natural Competitor

1. Brett Favre and Chris Havel, *Favre: For the Record.* New York: Doubleday, 1997, pp. 92, 93.
2. Favre and Havel, *Favre: For the Record,* p. 95.
3. Favre and Havel, *Favre: For the Record,* p. 98.
4. Quoted in Brett Favre and Bonita Favre, *Favre.* New York: Rugged Land, 2004, p. 180.
5. Favre and Havel, *Favre: For the Record,* p. 101.
6. Quoted in Favre and Favre, *Favre,* p. 180.
7. Favre and Havel, *Favre: For the Record,* p. 102.
8. Favre and Havel, *Favre: For the Record,* p. 111.
9. Favre and Favre, *Favre,* p. 199.
10. Favre and Havel, *Favre: For the Record,* p. 118.
11. Quoted in Beckett Publications, *Brett Favre Uncovered.* Dallas: Beckett, 1997, p. 77.
12. Quoted in Beckett Publications, *Brett Favre Uncovered,* p. 78.

Chapter 2: Struggles and Superstardom

13. Favre and Favre, *Favre,* p. 203.
14. Favre and Favre, *Favre,* p. 202.
15. Quoted in Mike Vandermause and Jeff Ash, eds., *Legendary: The Unforgettable Career of Brett Favre.* Green Bay, WI: Gannett Wisconsin News Paper Group, 2008, p. 75.
16. Favre and Havel, *Favre: For the Record,* p. 140.
17. Quoted in Vandermause and Ash, eds., *Legendary,* p. 75.
18. Quoted in *Appleton Post-Crescent,* "Brett Favre's 10 Most Memorable Games," March 9, 2008, p. 6.
19. Favre and Havel, *Favre: For the Record,* p. 144.
20. Quoted in *Appleton Post-Crescent,* "Brett Favre's 10 Most Memorable Games," p. 6.
21. Quoted in Peter King, "Warmed Up," *Sports Illustrated,* January 27, 1997, p. 70.
22. Quoted in King," Warmed Up," p. 70.

23. Quoted in *Appleton Post-Crescent*, "Brett Favre's 10 Most Memorable Games," p. 6.
24. Deanna Favre, *Don't Bet Against Me! Beating the Odds Against Cancer and in Life.* Carol Stream, IL: Tyndale House, 2007, p. 148.
25. Quoted in *Appleton Post-Crescent*, "Brett Favre's 10 Most Memorable Games," p. 6.

Chapter 3: From Rehab to the Super Bowl

26. Favre, *Don't Bet Against Me!,* p. 31.
27. Favre, *Don't Bet Against Me!,* p. 31.
28. Quoted in Peter King, "Bitter Pill," *Sports Illustrated,* May 27, 1996, p. 24.
29. Favre and Havel, *Favre: For the Record,* pp. 18, 30.
30. Favre and Havel, *Favre: For the Record,* p. 50.
31. Favre and Havel, *Favre: For the Record,* p. 64.
32. Favre and Havel, *Favre: For the Record,* p. 65.
33. Quoted in Favre, *Favre: For the Record,* p. 11.
34. Favre and Havel, *Favre: For the Record,* p. 174.
35. Favre and Havel, *Favre: For the Record,* p. 76.
36. Quoted in Vandermause and Ash, eds., *Legendary,* p. 105.
37. Favre and Havel, *Favre: For the Record,* p. 271.

Chapter 4: Disappointment and Frustration

38. Quoted in Packers.com, "Packers Lay Dallas 'Drought' to Rest, Regain NFC Central Lead," November 24, 1997. www.packers .com/news/releases/1997/11/11-24b.html.
39. Quoted in Michael Silver, "Second to None," *Sports Illustrated,* January 19, 1998, p. 30.
40. Quoted in Silver, "Second to None," p. 30.
41. Quoted in Peter King, "Merely Human," *Sports Illustrated,* February 2, 1998, p. 50.
42. Favre, *Don't Bet Against Me!,* p. 9.
43. Quoted in Vandermause and Ash, eds., *Legendary,* p. 117.
44. Quoted in Peter King, "Getting a Grip," *Sports Illustrated,* May 24, 1999, p. 74.
45. Quoted in King, "Getting a Grip," *Sports Illustrated,* May 24, 1999, p. 74.
46. Quoted in King, "Getting a Grip," p. 74.

Chapter 5: Triumph and Tragedy

47. Quoted in Peter King, "Thrown for a Loss," *Sports Illustrated,* September 4, 2000, p. 70.

48. Quoted in Jeff Blumb, ed., *Packers Media Guide.* Green Bay, WI: Green Bay Packers, 2005, p. 114.

49. Quoted in *Appleton Post-Crescent,* "Brett Favre's 10 Most Memorable Games," p. 6.

50. Quoted in Packers.com, "Packers Down Giants, Clinch Home Playoff Game," January 8, 2002. www.packers.com/news/releases/2002/01/01-08b.html.

51. Quoted in Packers.com, "Packers Wild Card Winners over San Francisco," January 15, 2002. www.packers.com/news/releases/2002/01/01-15b.html.

52. Favre and Favre, *Favre,* p. 31.

53. Favre and Favre, *Favre,* p. 47.

54. Quoted in Favre, *Don't Bet Against Me!,* p. 59.

55. Quoted in Peter King and David Sabino, "2 Green Bay Packers," *Sports Illustrated,* September 6, 2004, p. 140.

56. Quoted in *Appleton Post-Crescent,* "Brett Favre's 10 Most Memorable Games," p. 6.

Chapter 6: Record Player

57. Quoted in Dan Pompei, "Ripe for the Picking—But Far from Rotten," *Sporting News,* August 11, 2006, p. 48.

58. Tom Silverstein, "Green Bay Packers," *Sporting News,* January 13, 2006, p. 47.

59. Quoted in Dylan Tomlinson, "Favre Finally Commits After Three Months of Waiting," *Appleton Post-Crescent,* April 26, 2006, p. 4B.

60. Quoted in Dylan B. Tomlinson, "Favre Now Upbeat About Team's Talent," *Appleton Post-Crescent,* August 1, 2006, p. 5D.

61. Mike Woods, "To Return or Retire Is Something Only Favre Can Answer," *Appleton Post-Crescent,* January 1, 2007, p. 1B.

62. Quoted in Dylan Tomlinson, "Quarterback's Return Boosts Hopes for Season," *Appleton Post-Crescent,* February 3, 2007, p. 1A.

63. Quoted in Jon Krawczynski, "Favre Breaks Marino's Mark with 421st TD," ABC News, September 30, 2007. http://abcnews.go.com/Sports/wireStory?id=3671725.

64. Quoted in Mike Woods, "Packers Wise Not to Have Given Up on Favre," *Appleton Post-Crescent,* October 1, 2007, p. 1C.

65. Quoted in Peter King, "Top of the Charts," *Sports Illustrated,* October 8, 2007, p. 48.

66. Quoted in Jim Corbett, "Storming Back, Favre, Packers Plow On," *USA Today,* January 14, 2008, p. 5C.

67. Quoted in Jim Corbett, "Storming Back, Favre, Packers Plow On," p. 5C.

68. Quoted in Mike Spofford, "Game Review: NFC Title Slips Away," Packers.com, January 20, 2008. www.packers.com/news/stories/2008/01/20/6/.

69. Quoted in Mike Spofford, "Notebook: Driver's Big Play Can't Spark Offense," Packers.com, January 20, 2008. www.packers.com/news/stories/2008/01/20/5/.

70. Quoted in Alan Shipnuck, "Top of His Game," *Sports Illustrated,* March 17, 2008, p. 58.

71. Quoted in ESPN.com, "'Mentally Tired' Favre Tells Packers His Playing Career Is Over," March 5, 2008. http://espn.go.com/nfl/news/story?id=3276034.

72. Quoted in *Appleton Post-Crescent,* "I Know I Can Play, but I Don't Think I Want To," March 9, 2008, p. 11.

73. Quoted in *Appleton Post-Crescent,* "I Know I Can Play, but I Don't Think I Want To," p. 11.

74. Quoted in Associated Press, "Favre 'Comfortable' with Jets Following First Preseason Start," August 17, 2008. www.nfl.com/news/story;jsessionid=22DE0060C3D2861B89790167A4F77484?id=09000d5d80a130f2&template=with video&confirm=true.

1969

Brett Favre is born on October 10.

1987

Favre gets a scholarship to play football at Southern Mississippi. He starts as the seventh-string quarterback but soon becomes the starter.

1989

Favre's daughter Brittany is born.

1991

The Atlanta Falcons draft Favre on April 21.

1992

Favre is traded to the Green Bay Packers. He takes over as the team's quarterback after Don Majkowski is injured and starts his first game on September 27.

1995

Favre is named the NFL's Most Valuable Player; he is also selected as a Pro Bowl starter and is named the Performer of the Year by ESPN's ESPY Awards.

1996

Favre admits he is addicted to prescription painkillers and goes through rehab.

On July 14 he marries Deanna Tynes. He is again named the NFL's Most Valuable Player and is chosen as a Pro Bowl starter. Favre is also chosen as ESPN's Performer of the Year.

1997

In January Favre leads the Packers to a Super Bowl win over the New England Patriots.

For the third year in a row, Favre is chosen as the NFL's Most Valuable Player. He is also again named as the starting quarterback in the Pro Bowl.

1998

The Packers lose to the Broncos in the Super Bowl on January 25.

1999

Favre starts every game, despite having a nagging thumb injury. His daughter Breleigh is born.

2000

Favre throws his 250th career touchdown pass and is the second-fastest player in NFL history to reach that level.

2001

Favre is selected as the starting quarterback for the Pro Bowl for the fourth time in his career. He is the leading candidate in Pro Bowl fan balloting. On March 1, he signs a lifetime contract with the Packers.

2002

Sports Illustrated chooses Favre as Player of the Year, and he is again selected as a Pro Bowl starter.

2003

Favre delivers an amazing performance on Monday Night Football against the Oakland Raiders on December 22, the day after his father's death.

2005

Favre's childhood home is devastated by Hurricane Katrina, and he reaches out to flood victims by sending supplies.

2006

Favre becomes the NFL leader in pass completions.

2007

Favre sets records for most wins as a starting quarterback and most career NFL touchdown passes and pass attempts. He also sets a record for most NFL career passing yards. He is named *Sports Illustrated*'s Sportsman of the Year.

2008

Favre announces his retirement in March. That summer he decides to return to football, and is traded from the Packers to the New York Jets.

For More Information

Books

Brett Favre and Chris Havel, *Favre: For the Record*. New York: Doubleday, 1997. Favre frankly discusses his addiction to painkillers and talks about the team's 1996 Super Bowl–winning season in this autobiography.

Deanna Favre, *Don't Bet Against Me! Beating the Odds Against Breast Cancer and in Life*. Carol Stream, IL: Tyndale House, 2007. Deanna Favre talks about her fight against breast cancer and her life with her quarterback husband.

Sports Illustrated Books, *Brett Favre: The Tribute*. New York: Time, 2008. This book contains the *Sports Illustrated* articles written about Favre over the years. It also features many photos of the quarterback in action.

Periodicals

Dennis Dillon, "The Quarterback Next Door," *Sporting News,* March 17, 2008. A description of Favre, his career, and what he meant to the NFL.

Leigh Montville, "Leader of the Pack," *Sports Illustrated,* August 23, 1993. A look at Favre's first seasons as the Packers' quarterback.

Alan Shipnuck, "Sportsman of the Year," *Sports Illustrated,* December 10, 2007. Favre is honored for his work with charities and for his performance as a quarterback.

Alan Shipnuck, "Top of His Game," *Sports Illustrated,* March 17, 2008. This article talks about Favre's farewell to the NFL.

Steve Wulf, "Leaders of the Pack," *Time,* January 27, 1997. A look at Favre and the Packers and how the team brought glory back to Green Bay with a Super Bowl win.

Web Sites

NFL.com (www.nfl.com). This site contains a wealth of Favre's statistics.

Official Brett Favre Web Site (www.officialbrettfavre.com). This site offers comments from Favre as well as information on his charity. There is also a message board and a fan store.

Packers.com (www.Packers.com). Search the news archives for information on Favre's games as a Packer. The site also contains current information about the team.

Picture Credits

Cover, © Perlman, William/Star Ledger/Corbis
AP Images, 15, 25, 38, 40, 50, 55, 65, 69, 72, 76, 77, 80, 85
© Bettmann/Corbis, 27
Vernon Beiver/NFL/Getty Images, 41
Doug Collier/AFP/Getty Images, 53
Jonathan Daniel/Getty Images, 67
Tom Hauck/Allsport/Getty Images, 62
Allen Kee/NFL/Getty Images, 44
Kirby Lee/NFL/Getty Images, 31
Perry McIntyre/NFL/Getty Images, 25
Ronald C. Modra/Sports Illustrated/Getty Images, 11
Allen Steele/Getty Images Sport/Getty Images, 20
Tim Isbell/MCT/Landov, 12, 24
Reuters/Landov, 46
Allen Fredrickson/Reuters/Landov, 86
Eric Miller/Reuters/Landov, 7
Marc Serota/Landov, 19, 33, 57

Terri Dougherty has written dozens of books for children. Her parents have season tickets to the Packers games and raised her to be a Packers fan. Her favorite Favre moment was seeing him take time to meet with a young disabled child on the field before a game, kindly giving the child his full attention and looking like nothing else mattered at that moment.